Don't Freak Out!

HOME WORK

A Parent's Guide to Helping Out without Freaking Out

NEIL MCNERNEY, M.Ed., LPC

This Book Is Dedicated to My Wife
Colleen

Author's Important Links –Websites:
www.reducehomeworkstress.com
www.neilmcnerney.com
Email: neil@neilmcnerney.com

Contents

Introduction

I'd like to risk an assumption about why you are reading this book.

The biggest reason is because you love your kids. Regardless of how prepared you were for having kids, the amount of love you feel for them still surprises you. Because of that love, you want to do everything you can to help them be as successful in life as possible. So when you saw the title, you said to yourself, "If I can help my kid succeed in school, I'd like to know how."

But even though you love your kids, it's sometimes tough trying to help them be good students. It seems that sometimes, attempts you make to help them be successful backfire, either by direct defiance or a passive "I'll do it later."

Like most parents, you have promised yourself that you will be a better parent than the ones you had. You want to give your children everything they need to be a successful student. But doing everything you can to assure academic success seems to be backfiring. Maybe it's not going the way you thought it would. Maybe the more that you try to help, the worse it gets. Maybe it's helping your child, but ruining the great relationship you used to have. Homework time has become the most stressed-filled time of the day. Helping and being involved sometimes just causes more hard feelings and doesn't seem to improve things. You hope there is a better way to do all you can to help your kids be successful without exhausting yourself or harming your relationship with your kids. You are interested in reducing your own stress about homework so that you can enjoy your kids again.

About Me, Neil McNerney, LPC

When I read a book, especially a parenting book, I want to know a bit about the author. I ask myself: "Is this person credible? Do they have the credentials and experience to back up what they are saying?" If you are similar to me in this way, let me tell you a bit about myself:

I am a licensed professional counselor and have been licensed in the state of Virginia since 1994. I spent seven years as a school counselor, dealing with most of the issues in this book. I am on the teaching faculty of the Virginia Tech Graduate School of Marriage and Family Therapy, where I teach clinical techniques for working with children in a family context.

I speak and train nationally and regularly provide workshops and keynotes at state and national professional conferences. I have helped develop a parent training program that is being used by hundreds of professionals worldwide. The main focus of my work is increasing motivation in children and increasing the leadership skills of parents.

And, most importantly, my wife and I have two children, who constantly challenge my assumptions about parenting, especially when it comes to schoolwork. I am regularly amazed at the things they can accomplish on their own, and I am regularly challenged to use the right approach based on what is going on with them at the time.

What you will find in this book

A way to get rid of the constant cycle of worry, anger, temper, and guilt.

There is a reason why we are feeling more stressed, guiltier, and angrier than parents of previous generations. We have been sold a myth about parenting that doesn't create better kids but in fact tends to produce the very things we were trying to avoid. This book will help you understand these myths and provide a way to feel better about the way you are helping your child.

A refreshing, new way to look at your children's academics

There is a place between feeling anxious and responsible for your child's school work at one extreme, and cutting off and leaving it up to him on the other extreme. I will help you find this sometimes-elusive place, a place where you can be most effective as a parent.

A way to be an effective leader in your child's life that leaves you feeling good about your role in his life.

I will share an approach to helping your child that will leave you feeling good about your job as a parent, instead of feeling stressed and unsure. I will warn you: It's not an easy approach. It will require some work—and especially, self-control. But I assure you that the rewards will be worth it.

An approach to leading your student that has passed the test of time and professional scrutiny.

There tends to be two types of parenting books on the market. Some have very strong roots in the parenting profession. Books such as *1-2-3 Magic*, *Parenting with Love and Logic*, and *ScreamFree Parenting* are what professionals call "theoretically valid." They are based on proven theories of family systems and parent leadership. Other books, unfortunately, aren't so valid. As a teacher of the next generation of family therapists and parenting professionals, it is my obligation to make sure my book is not just helpful, but also stands up to the review of other professionals.

I have the pleasure of teaching at the Virginia Tech Graduate School of Marriage and Family Therapy, where my students are learning about family systems and becoming family therapists. When teaching some of the concepts about parent leadership, the students often ask: "Why don't parents know about this stuff? Why is it limited to graduate students?" Good question. This was one of the questions and challenges that led to me writing this book. The ideas I will share with you are effective, challenging, and theoretically solid. If the ideas were not grounded in a valid approach to family systems, my students would tear me up in an instant!

A way to lead our kids without it all being about the kids

I began working with families in 1988 as an elementary school counselor. I soon realized that my fascination was more about family dynamics than it was about working one-on-one with kids. So I went back to school and got a degree in family counseling.

During those early years (way way back in the 90's), I began to see this slow but steady shift in how we parent our children. The Self-Esteem movement had begun in earnest, with the main concept being: If we can help a child feel good about himself, he will do better in life. We began focusing more and more energy on helping kids feel good, in hopes that they would then have the self-confidence to face challenges and be more successful.

Our focus became about the children. Teachers, parents, schools, everyone became very child focused. I should have started a bumper sticker company around then, because this was the time when we began to emblazon our cars with great things about our kids. Honor roll students, student of the week, winning school sports teams, and so on were made into stickers for everyone to see. Soon, everyone knew how well our kids were doing in school and what sports they were excelling at, just by looking at the back of our cars.

Our goal was to make our kids feel good about themselves. Nothing wrong with that, right? But then an interesting thing began to happen. We, the parents, started to blur the line between our kids' accomplishments and our own accomplishments. We have told the world (or at least our neighborhood) what great kids we have. "Look at the great things my kids are doing," is what we are saying. It was our cars that sported the bumper stickers, not their bicycles or their backpacks. We, the parents, were the ones shouting the great news.

But then, we began to feel the pressure to keep it up. We started to look at every little slip as a possible worry point. Instead of focusing on how we could be a leader, we began to get more and more involved, increasing our own worry, and causing more conflict at home.

I remember a story a mother told me about how hard it is to not take it personally. "It seems every time I am running errands and run into a friend, she tells me about how great her kids are doing. When she asks me how Alex is doing, I want to make up a story. I'm concerned that if I tell her the truth, she will wonder what I'm doing wrong."

This is a feeling that most parents have. It is so hard not to take it personally. The mother continued: "It gets worse when, if I do share that Alex is having difficulties, they begin giving advice. It's worse because I sometimes hear opposing pieces of advice. I have been told to be more strict, and I have also been told to be more lenient and let Alex figure this out. I don't know what to do."

If I told you that I don't feel the same worries as this mom, I would be lying. When my kids are doing well academically, everything is happiness and rainbows. But let one paper come home that looks like a stumble, and I start to feel those same worries. I start to take my kids' work personally.

It was at that point, just a few years ago, that I happened to come across a book called *ScreamFree Parenting*. The author, Hal Runkel, put in writing what I have been slowly coming to grips with: When we become too child-focused, we lose our sense of self and end up taking our kid's ups and downs too personally. I have worked with Hal and The ScreamFree Institute for the past three years developing a professional training model that helps parents stay calm and connected. We have had the good fortune to touch the lives of thousands of parents and train hundreds of professionals, especially on U.S. military bases and posts throughout the world.

The Parent's Dilemma - Too Little, Too Much

There are many dilemmas we face when it comes to parenting our kids. If we do too little, we might end up being neglectful. Our kids won't get all of the opportunities, structure, and discipline necessary to do well in life. If we do too much, we run the risk of decreasing their internal motivation.

We run the risk of increasing our resentment, anger, and worry. And we run the risk of them actually doing worse in school.

Our goal is to find that "just right approach" that provides leadership but doesn't produce resentment. But in order to do that, we are faced with one dilemma after another.

I had to Google the word "dilemma" to make sure I was using the right word. Instead of giving you Webster's definition, I'll use the first definition that came up on the Internet. It was from, of course, Wikipedia:

A dilemma (Greek: δί-λημμα "double proposition") is a problem offering at least two possibilities, neither of which is practically acceptable.

Dilemmas are the one constant thing we deal with as parents. They come up over and over again. Take, for instance, trust. I discuss this issue in detail in Chapter 9. Our kids want to be trusted. We want to trust them. But they keep being sneaky, and sometimes boldly lying to us. Here's the dilemma: "If I trust you more, you will just lie again and again. If I don't trust you, there will always be tension between us. I will always have my detective badge on, and you will always feel like a suspect."

Sometimes dilemmas can go away, just by thinking about the issue in a bit of a different way. I am going to teach you how to look at a problem a bit differently.

I remember what a student told me once about seeing things differently. He was ten years old at the time. He and his parents were working with me on increasing his focus and motivation in school. Things had gone well and we were finishing up the counseling process. It was our last session, and we were reviewing what went well. The first thing he said was that he had begun looking at his problems differently than before. "In what way?" I asked him. "Well, whenever me and my mom and dad would come in with a problem, we were always looking at the problem front-ways." I wasn't sure what "front-ways" meant, but I didn't want to interrupt. He continued: "And then you would say something or ask a question that made us look at the problem different. It was like you were looking at the problem side-ways. Instead of front-ways."

"How did that help?" I asked. I wasn't exactly clear yet what he meant, so I was stalling for time.

"When we started looking at the problem side-ways, we were able to see new answers instead of just the problem," he said.

Now I got it. I was impressed. This ten-year-old had just captured what I try to do for kids and families: change how they see the problem. If we change how we see problems, solutions are just around the corner—or side street.

I will be asking you to look a bit differently at the problems you are having with your kid's schoolwork. I will be asking you to do the same about how you are trying to deal with these problems. Your goal in picking up this book is to learn new ideas and new tools to help increase your child's school success. If that is what you are looking for, you will be pleased. This book is not a rehash of what has been said in the past by many competent educators and parent specialists. This is a new look at the problem, and a new look at the solutions.

A Few Words of Caution

1. *Don't try to change too much too quickly.* Looking at problems in a different manner, side-ways, can be a bit unsettling. The ideas in this book will stretch you and make you a stronger leader in your child's life. But remember: becoming stronger is hard work and often causes soreness at first. Just like trying anything new, it will get easier with time and practice.

2. *Avoid "Yes, but" thoughts.* "Yes, but" thoughts are those thoughts that get in the way of trying new things. They are a way for us to say, "Yes, I understand what you are saying, and it makes complete sense. But it won't work." It puts us in a closed-mind situation very quickly. If we are

to improve the success of our children, it's pretty important to avoid the "Yes, buts" as much as possible. Here are a few ways it might show up in your mind:

a. *I tried that. It didn't work.* There is a possibility that you have tried some of the suggestions in this book. I am pretty certain that most of the ideas will be new to you, or the way I will suggest you use the idea will be different than the past. In either case, try to avoid dismissing an idea because it hasn't worked in the past. One of the main reasons some approaches didn't work in the past is because there was some secondary benefit your kid was getting from the situation. The main secondary benefit for our kids: Our emotional reactivity. The more we freak out, the worse things get. The calmer we become, the more student success is possible.

b. *That would never work with my child.* Don't bet on it. If I had a nickel for every time I have heard a parent say, "That wouldn't work for my child," I would be rich. Well, not exactly rich (it takes a lot of nickels to be rich), but I'd have enough money for a nice dinner for my family! When it comes to your child, don't assume that you have her figured out and know what might work and what might not work. You might be surprised.

c. *My kid has special needs. That won't work for special needs kids.* I have developed these ideas of parent leadership with the help of hundreds of special needs students and their parents. Some ideas might have to be adjusted a bit for your child, but the concepts will still be effective regardless of the need. This is not a book about differentiated instruction, or any specific educational approach. This is a book about how we can tap into those basic desires that all kids have: A desire for success, a desire to make others proud, and a desire to be trustworthy. I will help you find ways to help your child make those desires a reality.

d. *That idea doesn't match with my parenting philosophy.* Preconceived ideas sometimes get in our way. But in actuality, there are no such things as preconceived ideas. We were not born with these parenting ideas. We conceived them as some point after taking in lots of information. All I am asking you to do is to take in additional information that might change your conception of your job as a parent.

3. *Change is hard, especially on you. Adjust your life accordingly.* In Chapter 11, you will learn about the willpower fuel tank, a powerful new way to look at willpower that explains a lot about why change is hard to sustain and why students have difficulty maintaining focus. Until you read that chapter, remember this: Try to simplify your life a bit while attempting to make these changes. If you can, reduce the number of challenges you face so that you have the willpower to try a different approach.

So try to keep these ideas in mind as you read the book. I think it will greatly improve your chances for success.

And although it goes without saying, your kids are worth it.

CHAPTER ONE

Don't Freak Out!

Why Staying Calm Does Wonders

One of the best ways to help your child be successful in school is to be under control. You notice that I didn't use the term "in control," but "under control." The difference is huge. By under control, I mean that **you** are in control **of yourself**, instead of someone else being in control.

When you are under control, you are saying that, regardless of what grades come home, regardless of how much homework gets done; you will decide how you feel and how you react. The benefits of staying calm, regardless of what happens, are many:

"When we stay calm...we keep the focus on our child."

Why do we want our kids to do well in school? Seems a pretty obvious question. We want our kids to do well so that they will be successful. When we can stay calm, we are increasing the odds of success. The calmer I am, the more likely my kids' energies will be focused on their own actions instead of mine.

If I am not calm, their thoughts and emotions are focused on me. The message, when I am not calm, is this: Calm me down (Runkel, 2007). So, instead of thinking about doing well in school for their own success, they think they should do well in school to change our emotions.

When we are over-anxious or losing our temper, we have lost a chance to help with self- motivation.

I remember a teenager I worked with who was struggling in school. Every time he missed a homework assignment or got a bad test grade, his mother went ballistic. When I would ask him why he wanted to do well in school, he would tell me "so that Mom won't yell at me." When I would ask if there were other reasons, he would just shrug. All he was focused on was doing well to calm his mother. So what do you think happened when he went away to college? You guessed it. He lasted one semester and dropped out with failing grades. He told me: "When I went to college, it was great! I was having fun, meeting new people, and the biggest part was not having Mom yell at me and check my home-work all the time. The problem, though, was that I never really learned to study in order to be successful. The only reason I studied was to get Mom off my back."

So when Mom was not around anymore, neither was his motivation to do well. He never learned self-motivation, only how to manage his mother's moods.

When we send the message to our kids that it's their job to calm us down, it sometimes makes the immediate situation better (like the story you just read), but doesn't make any long-term change. Sometimes, though, it will have the exact opposite effect and make things worse. There are some kids who deal with this type of message very differently. Instead of rising to the occasion and working to calm their parents, they will do the exact opposite, guaranteeing that the parents will get even more upset and angry.

"Don't Rattle My Cage!!"

I have a small zoo not far from where I live. It was a great zoo because our kids could get really close to the animals. In one section, they had a large cage about the size of a small house, and it was filled with monkeys. These monkeys were pretty excitable, so about every six feet the owners had posted signs saying: "Please Do Not Rattle The Cage." So, of course, whenever a group of boys came by and saw that sign, you know exactly what they did. They rattled the cage. The sign was like a major invitation to the boys. They had to see what would happen, even though I'm sure they had a good idea that the monkeys would go nuts. And that's exactly what did happen. A boy would pick up a stick, rattle it against the bars, and the monkeys would go nuts.

Some kids view our own temper as parents in the same way. They get a bit of power out of being able to rattle our cage. Some kids, especially kids that have little motivation to do well in school, have given up trying to make their parents proud and instead focus on making them angry. "You get that upset over a C? Let's see what you do when I bring home an F." It's the proverbial cutting off their nose to spite their face. But in this case they are giving you the exact opposite of what you want just to spite you. They will give you the exact opposite of what you want just to prove that they cannot be controlled.

Especially with kids like this, staying calm can be very powerful. When we take our emotions out of the equation, they don't have anything to push against. If I, by being calm, send the message "I am going to be calm, regardless of how you do in school," I take away a huge motivating factor for underachieving. I have taken away the thing that they are rebelling against.

"When we stay calm...it feels much, much better."

I have never, ever felt better after losing my temper with my kids. Sure, I feel a bit of a release immediately after, but that feeling goes away very quickly. It's then replaced with guilt, regret, remorse, you name a negative feeling, and I'm probably feeling it. Sometimes I'll try to justify my actions by saying "Well, he deserved it." But I don't really believe that.

There has been some very compelling research about what happens to us when we lose our temper. It used to be thought that losing our temper was a type of "release." That we were releasing the pressure, which would lead to calm. We used to think that if we bottled up our emotions, it would somehow be bad for us.

But recent research is actually telling us the opposite. In our brains, we have two major types of mood chemicals: endorphins and cortisols. Endorphins are the good mood chemicals. They helps us relax, stay focused, decrease pain, and lots of other good stuff. Cortisols tend to do the opposite. They are released during stressful times and increase blood pressure, decrease mood, increase inflammation, and other not-so-good stuff.

When we lose our temper, the amount of endorphins being released in our brains decreases, and the amount of cortisols increases. The increase has been show to last up to four hours after someone loses his temper. So for four hours after I lose my temper, it's pretty likely that I'll actually feel worse, not just because of guilt and regret, but because I just shot my brain with a big dose of bad mood.

"When we stay calm...we keep the focus on the child, not us."

Think about the last three times you have lost your temper about schoolwork. Go ahead and write down what you did or said each of those times:

1. _____

2. _____

3. _____

Now, think about what probably was going on in your child's head after each of your outbursts. I would predict that, when we lose our temper, it is pretty likely that our child's focus is now on us, not on himself. When I lose my cool with my kids, I have given them the option to no longer look at their own issues, but to look at my issues instead. If I yell: "Go upstairs and do your homework!" he might actually go upstairs, but instead of thinking about getting the work done, he will be thinking about what a jerk he has for a father. Instead of telling himself, "I've got to get this done," he will ask himself "Why is my dad so worried about school all the time?" Whenever we lose our temper, we have taken away a chance for us to lead.

A true leader is a motivator. Actually, a true leader is someone who can help foster self-motivation. When our kids do their schoolwork because they are worried about how we will react, they are certainly motivated. But they are "other-motivated," not "self-motivated." An other-motivated student has to be continually pushed to get work done and stay on task. A self-motivated student learns how to keep the motivation going without having to rely on someone else's actions to jump-start it. We are much more able to instill self-motivation by being calm than by being reactive.

What kind of wake do I want to leave?

The first time I heard someone ask this question, I thought they meant "wake" as in funeral. But it was actually referring to the wake a boat leaves. When a boat moves through the water, it leaves a series of waves behind it, called a wake. Up to a point, the faster a boat travels, the bigger a wake it leaves. There are places that have signs that say, "No Wake Zone," because a boat's wake can cause damage to the shore, damage to anchored boats, and can actually capsize canoes.

When I am calm, there's a pretty good chance I will leave a calm wake behind me. When I am not calm, my wake might cause some damage. I love this quote from Maya Angelou:

"I've learned that people will forget what you said, people will forget what you did, but people will never forget how you made them feel."

How to Stay Calm:

OK, Neil. Stay Calm. But that is easier said than done. It's actually **much** easier said than done. I'll put it right up there with some of my other easy to say and hard to do suggestions like eating right and exercising regularly. In order to stay calm we've got to look at what is churning us up in the first place.

Get Control of Your Worries

I would suggest that almost all of our feelings that cause us trouble when it comes to our kids' schoolwork is based on one emotion: worry.

Worry is a good emotion at times, especially when it activates us to do something different about our actions. For example, if I am worried that a project is not as good as it could be for work, my worry could motivate me to spend more time on it to make it better. If I'm worried that I haven't been paying enough attention to my wife, it could lead me to taking her out to dinner. So worries can be good, but only when we focus on ourselves and the worry lead us to change OUR actions.

But most of our worries, when it comes to schoolwork, are not based on our actions. Our worries are based on our kids' actions (or lack of). We worry about how their actions will affect their future. And often times we allow our worries to go unchecked, which will lead us to the "My child is going to live in my basement forever" thoughts.

SUGGESTION: Put a Fence Around Your Worries

Just like most dogs need a fence in order to stay where we want them to stay, our worries need a fence as well. If we don't put a fence around our worries, then we have lost control of them—and who knows what type of havoc they might cause at that point and beyond?

⌷ SUGGESTION: Create a Pause Between Action ○ and Reaction

Step 1 - What are your pre-temper indicators?

Think about yourself for a moment: What might be the first indications that you are getting ready to blow? Think about whether it might be a thought, an emotion, a physical sensation, or something else. For me, I notice that I begin to shake my head, like "I can't believe you just did that!" I will also sigh pretty loudly and then often say my kid's name in an unflattering tone!

What about your indicators? Write down the three things that happen inside when you are beginning to feel like you might lose your temper:

1. _____

2. _____

3. _____

My next suggestion is to write these three things down on a small card and keep it with you for the next week. Whenever you notice the card, review the three pre-temper indicators. The more that you take the time to remember what they are, the more likely you will be able to take the next step.

Step 2 - Pause

When you notice that your pre-temper indicators are happening, stop whatever you are doing. Don't say anything. Don't do anything. OK, if you are driving a car, keep driving! But wait, wait, wait, and don't say anything to your child at that moment.

For example, you are driving home from practice and are almost home when you child says: "Oh, by the way, I need to get some poster board for a project that's due tomorrow." Instead of yelling, "You're telling me this now???" just pause. Keep driving and wait until you have gotten completely calm before you decide how to respond. The only way you will be able to know which leadership style to use in this particular situation is by being calm. So take the time and calm down first.

Don't Freak Out Summary

There is no denying it: We are better leaders when we are calm. It's our responsibility to keep ourselves calm, not our child's responsibility.

The two ways to keep your worries under control:

1. Put a fence around your worries
2. Pause between action and reaction

Don't Freak Out Resources

One of the best ways to get the most out of this book is to personalize the information for your particular situation. I have added additional information online that can help you make the most of this book. For instance, I have developed a way to set goals for change. Go to

www.reducehomeworkstress.com/exercises/fence

for an exercise in putting a fence around your worries. On this web page, I will help you determine what your major worries are when it comes to your child; develop a strategy to stay calm, and a way to remind yourself of your goal.

CHAPTER TWO

What Kind of Parent Are You?

This chapter might seem a bit odd at first glance. For goodness sakes, you are reading this book to help find ways to help your child. I am sure you were expecting more information about your children by this point. But instead of beginning by focusing on our kids, I want you to begin by taking a look at yourself.

Oddly enough, most parenting books say very little about the parents, but instead are focused on techniques to change your kids' behavior. I am going to ask you to spend a bit of time thinking about yourself. When you understand yourself, your ability to help them be successful in school, and life, is going to increase dramatically.

The Typical Parenting Styles

When I first had kids, I began to read about parenting styles. There was not much out there at the time, and most of it focused on three major styles: authoritarian, permissive, and authoritative. These are the typical parenting styles that people have used for decades[1]. I like to nickname them the Goldilocks styles: Too Hard, Too Soft, and Just Right.

Authoritarian (Too Hard) – This is the drill sergeant, "Because I said so!" approach. No explanations are given. There is little to no flexibility in rules and the punishments tend to be harsh. The main thing that children tend to learn from this style is that pleasing the parent is the most important issue. They tend to have a harder time learning why behaving a certain way is a good thing. Kids raised this way tend to be both obedient and skilled in life, or they become very rebellious. Either way, they report less happiness than kids raised with the other styles.

Permissive (Too Soft) – Permissive parents tend to be somewhat nontraditional and extremely nurturing. They put very few demands on their kids and rarely use discipline. "Talking it out" is the main way of dealing with problems and misbehavior. They tend to be very lenient. When rules are broken, there are usually no consequences. Kids raised this way tend to be pretty unhappy as adults with the added bonus of having more difficulty with authority figures, including teachers.

Authoritative (Just Right) – I wish we could use a different word for this style instead of one that is so similar to the "Too Hard" style. Sometimes people call this "Democratic." A Just Right parent has clear rules that children should follow, but is able to be more flexible and take in other information before deciding on an appropriate response. They are able to stay calm and provide a stable place for children to learn how to be successful in life.

To be honest, despite our best intentions, most of us as parents occasionally demonstrate characteristics of all three styles, right? But let's see where you think you predominantly reside:

Parenting Style Quiz

This little quiz will help you figure out which parenting style you tend to use with your child. Please pick only one child for this exercise, preferably the one you struggle with the most. Read the bold sentence and then pick which response you would likely use. Don't try to figure out which is the "right" answer, just pick which one you know you would probably say. Add up your points as you go along.

You ask your child what the homework looks like for tonight and she says, "I don't know. I'll deal with it later."

1. You immediately punish her for the implied back talk and also tell her she will do the homework now. (1 Point)

2. You ask her: "When is 'later'? I would like to know how much you have so I can plan the evening." (2 Points)

3. You say, "OK, dear. I know you will, dear…" (3 Points)

Your son comes home with a D+ on a test. He has been getting poor grades for a while in this class.

1. You ground him for the weekend and take away his electronics without having any conversation about what happened and simply tell him he needs to focus. (1 Point)

2. You talk with him about what happened and think about what punishment/response would be helpful in this situation. (2 Points)

3. You tell him he is smart and you're sure he will do better next time. (3 Points)

He then tells you that the teacher stinks and everybody got bad grades. Then he says, "I wasn't even going to tell you because I knew you'd freak out."

1. You ground him for the weekend, take away the electronics, and make him clean his room for being disrespectful. (1 Point)

2. You talk with him about what happened. You decide to ignore his attempt at blaming the teacher and you, and instead focus on how he felt about his preparation, and why he thinks he received a D+. (2 Points)

3. You ask him about the other students and his teacher, but do not directly discuss his feelings about the test. (3 Points)

Results:

Now, add up your points to see which type of parenting style you tend to use:

- **3–4 points.** You are in the Too Hard Zone. Rules are very important to you and strictness is a good thing. Although you might get short-term compliance, the relationship is beginning to suffer and long-term performance is not good.

- **5–7 points**. You are in the Just Right Zone, or the sweet spot. You have found a way to stay in the middle during tough times and can stay focused even when your child is trying to use excuses.

- **8–9 points**. You are probably in the Too Soft Zone. Nurturing is extremely important to you, and you hope it will be enough. But you are worried that it isn't because things aren't getting better.

When you consider these three styles, it's clear that the experts encourage the authoritative approach. Everything I read was clear: If I parented this way, my kids would be well-adjusted, have good friends, behave well, get good grades, clean their rooms, and possibly win a Nobel Prize. Sounds good, right? I thought so. But in reality, the type of parent we are and the style we most commonly use is a reflection of years of cultivation, both conscious and subconscious. To the point, there is generally a disconnect between the type of parent we think we are and what actually comes out during the times of stress—the times that really count. The hardest part of this process is actually being that type of parent we need to be when the problems hit the fan, when we are tired, or frustrated, or overwhelmed.

When my son Max began middle school, it seemed everything was going well. He had a great time in elementary school and had very good grades. We knew that middle school would be different and were confident that he would adjust well to all the changes: multiple teachers, new students, lockers, harder work, etc.

Everything began very well. He loved meeting new kids and was actually happy with almost all of his teachers. My wife and I breathed a sigh of relief and thought that this was going to go just fine. And it did go fine. But "going fine" also means that there are many adjustments—some of which were difficult for Max, as they would be for any kid. He began, as most middle schoolers do, to have difficulty keeping it all straight. Sometimes schoolwork was missing or forgotten. I didn't notice it at the time, but I later noticed that as Max's worries about school increased, so did mine. What did I do with my worries? I would get annoyed and angry with him.

And I'm supposed to be an expert at this.

I remember one morning vividly. It was about ten minutes before he was to go to the bus stop and he quietly came to me and asked, "Dad, can you take me to school today instead of the bus?" I was on full alert right away. You see, the bus takes about 45 minutes to reach the school. I can drive him there in 15 minutes. Why did he need that extra half hour? When I asked why, he told me exactly what I was assuming. He had forgotten to do some homework the previous night and wanted to get it done right now.

This was the last straw! My questions were rapid-fire, like a cross examination. "Do you remember me asking you if you had done all your homework? Did you see this assignment when I told you to check your assignment book? Or did you just want to keep watching TV? Wait, get back here!"

I made this last demand because he had quietly left the room while I was ranting—and I didn't even know it! "Fine. I don't care. Let him learn his lesson." These were the thoughts going on in my angry head.

I was NOT being the Just Right parent during that lousy parenting moment. I had let my emotions, my anger, and my worry get in the way, to the point that my son wanted nothing to do with me. Simply telling myself, "I'll be the Just Right parent," style is not enough. I had to find out what was getting in my way of being a good leader during the hard times so that I could stay calm and connected when it mattered most.

Real-Life Parenting Styles

Though the original trio of typical parenting styles is a good place to start, I don't think it helps us become the best parents we can be, especially when we are exhausted, worried, and fed up. I realized that it is not about being one type of parent all the time. It is about recognizing the situation at any given time and responding with the appropriate style. Like my situation with Max, it's easy for me to say, as if I am choosing from a menu: "Let's see…I think I'll pick the Authoritative style." But staying in that style is the hard part. The key to being the best parent we can be lies in understanding how we react when we are under stress and how we can stay in the style we choose, even when stressed out.

By asking yourself, "What kind of parent am I?" I am asking you to look at how you deal with the tough times of parenting. When things are going well at my house, and my kids are getting their homework done nice and quietly, I am the best dad in the world. But what about the tough times, when homework isn't getting done, the TV won't stay turned off, and the back talk is bubbling up? That's the time I would like you to consider which of these parenting styles to use.

As you read through these, you will probably see some of yourself in many, if not all of them. That's OK. In fact, that's pretty normal and ideal. The goal of taking a look at this is to understand yourself a little better when it comes to managing the trials and tribulations that your child's schooling will inevitably bring. Below is your parenting style toolbox. At any given time, one or more of the styles will suit any situation you need to address with your student.

The Calm Parent

Let's start with the one we all would like to strive toward: The Calm Parent. This is the person who can deal with whatever comes her way with a calm demeanor. She doesn't take bad grades personally, so she doesn't allow herself to get angry or anxious about it. She realizes that her children's actions are rarely directed at her, so there is no need to get emotional. She's the parent we all strive to be.

The Anxious Parent

Almost all of our feelings that cause us trouble when it comes to our kids' school work are based on one emotion: Worry. Call it fear, call it anxiety. It's all the same. It's that lousy feeling we get when we think about how things might end up in the future. We don't worry about the past. Worry is about the future. Have you ever found yourself going down the following path?

- If she doesn't do this homework assignment, she's going to get a zero on it.

- If she doesn't start doing her homework, she's going to fail.

- If she fails, it's going to affect her GPA.

- If she has a bad GPA, she won't get into a good college.

- She might not get into *any* college.

- If she doesn't get into college, how can she get a good job?

- If she doesn't get a good job, she'll be living in my basement forever!

What do all of these thoughts have in common? They are all about the future. Our worries are about what MIGHT happen in the future. The problem with this worry is that it has to do with someone else's actions, not our actions.

Our anxiety, when we give it free rein, can really affect our kids. The problem is that the effect is rarely positive. Our kids might do their homework quicker, but the reason they are getting it done is to reduce our anxiety. When we are freaking out about their homework, we are telling them to do it to keep me calm.

The biggest problem with being anxious about our kids is that anxiety is extremely contagious. Our anxiety will quickly become our kids' anxiety. So even if our anxiety gets reduced, our kids' anxieties will increase, sometimes to unhealthy levels.

The Angry Parent

Believe it or not, there is not much difference between the Angry Parent and the Anxious Parent. It is the way that the worry comes out that makes a difference. Where the anxious parent hovers, the angry parent yells. While the anxious parent checks every five minutes to see if homework is getting done, the angry parent assumes the worst and punishes immediately.

Do you remember the story of the student from chapter one that tried to do well in school just to get his mother off his back? When I would ask him why he wanted to do well in school, he would tell me "so that Mom won't yell at me." He never learned to study and do well for himself. Instead, he only did it for his mom.

When we send the message to our kids that it's their job to calm us down, it sometimes makes the immediate situation better (like the story you just read), but doesn't make any long-term change. Sometimes, though, it will have the exact opposite effect and make things worse. There are some kids who deal with their parent's freaking out very differently. Instead of rising to the occasion and working to calm their parents, they will do the exact opposite, guaranteeing that the parents will get even more upset and angry.

The Supportive Parent

This parent's main role is to be a support for his children. He assumes that his kids want to do well in school, so he looks for opportunities to praise. He is quick to be sympathetic when bad grades come home and tries to avoid giving advice unless he is asked. A supportive parent is a style that is good to learn, but it is even more important to understand when and when not to use it. For example, the supportive parent works for students who are pretty responsible. By being supportive, they hear from us, "You can do well. I believe you can do it." This support is very helpful for them.

I recently worked with a student whose mother was great at using supportive language. He is a good student who occasionally had trouble staying on top of assignments. During one particularly tough time, when he was falling a bit behind, his mother told him: "I know you can get caught up. I've seen you do it before and I know you can do it again. Let me know if you need any help." Her comments were non-judgmental, calm, and confident. That was exactly what this student needed to feel: that he had the ability to get caught up.

On the other hand, the student who is lying and being defiant doesn't benefit very much from the parent who is only being supportive.

For example, if a student is caught cheating, it's probably not the time to say supportive comments like "I know you really wanted to do well." At least it wouldn't be appropriate to only be supportive. A kid caught cheating needs some additional leadership from you so that he won't cheat again. Being supportive alone, without any other style, wouldn't be helpful.

The Blaming Parent

This is the parenting style we use when we are completely fed up with someone. And when you are dealing with your child's schoolwork, there are plenty of places to lay blame. When it comes to school issues, the Four S's are:

Self - It's my fault that I can't find a way to get the work done!

Student - He's not taking this seriously.

School - They are giving too much homework.

Society - There's too much pressure on kids these days.

The problem with blaming, however, is that it usually does nothing to make things better. Blame yourself and you will just feel even more guilty. Blame the student and he will try to place the blame elsewhere. Blame the school and they will either get defensive or tell you that this is just the way we do things. Blame society and, well, nothing happens since society is not something that can respond.

A parent who blames others for problems will very quickly produce a child who blames others for her problems. Our kids pick up these things very quickly. When a child is constantly exposed to a blaming parent, she learns that "It's not my fault. It's someone else's fault." This, obviously, is not a good thing. We want our kids to be in control of their own actions and path in life. When we teach them to blame others, we teach them that other people control their destiny.

When we spend a lot of time trying to find someone to blame, we teach our kids that the first thing to do is to find who is at fault, instead of trying to figure out a solution. "But what if I am blaming my child?" The problem with blaming our children is that very few kids will hear: "It's your fault," and be able to agree and say: "That's right. It's my fault."

The Consultant

The Consultant is more active than the Supporter. When your role is the Consultant, you are still being the Supporter, plus you are adding information and advice. You have given your child the chance to try to be successful on his own, but there are still some things getting in the way. So you add some advice that might be accepted.

The goal of the Consultant is to give advice that will be heard. The challenge for the Consultant is to find the right time to give advice, which might not be at the moment something is happening. A good time to give advice is usually after things have calmed down and schoolwork is put away. The worst time is any time the student is upset, anxious, or angry.

The Perfectionist

The Perfectionist likes to have things…perfect. If you are a perfectionist, it has probably worked out for you very well throughout your life. As a child, you probably did well in school and at home. In most areas, your perfectionism has been rewarded.

The place where perfectionism needs to be carefully finessed is at home, especially when it comes to our kids. We tend to make the classic perfectionist's mistake:

Instead of focusing our perfectionism on ourselves, we begin to focus it on others. Instead of trying to find the way to be the best parent we can be, we focus on having the best kid we can have. So instead of looking at our own actions and measuring how close they are to perfect, we begin to measure kids actions to see how close they are to perfect.

One of the problems with this is the fact that it is pretty likely that your child is nowhere near the perfectionist you are. It is almost guaranteed that he isn't. So if we focus on trying to make our kids as perfect as us, we will always be disappointed.

But all is not lost! If you do have the perfectionist streak, your best bet is to focus it inward instead of outward. How can I be the best parent I can be? What would the perfect parent do in this situation?

Now, I am not suggesting that you be the perfect parent. It is impossible. All I am suggesting is that you turn that energy toward someone you can actually control: yourself.

The effect of perfectionism on students is pretty universal: They feel they will never measure up. Unless they perform at 100 percent intensity and achievement, they have failed.

Kids tend to react to the Perfectionist parent in two ways. Unfortunately, neither one is very healthy. The first way is for the kid to become perfectionistic herself. I recently worked with a high school girl who couldn't get herself to school unless all of her work was perfect. For her, it was either perfection or nothing. So if she hadn't completed all of her work perfectly, she wouldn't go to school.

On the other side of the spectrum, are the kids who have been come to this conclusion: "If I can't measure up, even if I try really hard, I might as well stop trying. If my parents are going to be disappointed in me anyway, I should probably have some fun at least."

My work with families is filled with students like this. They haven't given up on life, but they have given up on trying to win the approval of their parents.

The Boss

The Boss is a very important role. The Boss is the parent who is still trying to be supportive, and is also trying to be a consultant, with the added "teeth" of being able to hand out consequences. When you are the Boss, you have realized that your child, for whatever reason, needs a bit more "oomph" to be motivated.

The Boss is able to calmly assess the situation and determine what is the minimum reward or punishment that might tilt things toward action.

Unfortunately, we tend to jump to The Boss role way too quickly. It is a powerful tool if used right, but when we use some of the other roles first, using the Boss role might have more beneficial long-term effects.

These are the real-life roles we play when it comes to schoolwork. As parents, some of these roles can be very effective. Timing, however, is crucial. Timing is dictated by how our kids are managing any given situation. Some of these roles, however, don't tend to be helpful at any time. Later in the book I will be focusing on the three most effective of these styles and helping you figure out when to use which style.

But I think it is beneficial to begin thinking about yourself first and your own natural tendencies.

Don't Freak Out Summary

- You have complete control over how to successfully parent through any challenge.
- The first step is to identify the type of parent you naturally are.
- Decide what adjustments you can make to be more effective.
- Assess each situation individually and choose the Authentic Parenting Style best suited for the moment.

Don't Freak Out Exercise

For the quiz on being too soft, too hard, or just right go to:
www.reducehomeworkstress.com/exercises/just-right

Don't Freak Out Resource

For a listing of the types of real-life parenting styles and why they might or might not work, go to:
www.reducehomeworkstress/exercises/real-life-styles

CHAPTER THREE

Decoding Our Kids

In this chapter, I want to help you understand your kids better. There are a number of ways that students deal with schoolwork, and it is important for us as parents figure out what ways our particular kid deals with it. I am going to call these "Styles." I like the term because, like many other styles, it changes from time to time and even from day to day! Our kid's homework style can also change that quickly.

This step, understanding the homework style, is an important piece of the C.A.L.M. Method. The C.A.L.M. approach will be detailed in Chapter 6. In order to help our kids, we need to understand what's happening with them. Each student style has an approach that will work best. So our ability to pick the best approach is based on understanding accurately which style our kid is showing.

Just like we take on certain roles as parents, some good and some not-so-good, our kids take on certain roles as students. When we can identify those roles, it becomes much easier to decide how to help them and lead them.

When you read through these different styles, keep in mind that one child can have many different styles depending on the year, or even the day. Your child can also have more than one style during the same time! For instance, she might be the responsible student when it comes to math, but she is the unmotivated student for science.

In Chapter 5, I will give you some specific advice about how to lead each type. I have found some very effective ways that can increase motivation and success, but I want you to get it after I have shared with you some other important pieces of the puzzle. I will describe each role and then give you a bit of information about the ups and downs of being this style.

The Responsible Student

The Responsible Student is able to find the right balance, the sweet spot, between getting all the work done on time and not overdoing it. She takes school seriously, but doesn't overly stress about it. Homework assignments are usually written in the assignment notebook and finished on time just about every day. She feels good about her work and only stresses during stressful times: big tests, finals, project due dates. Usually, most kids have one or two subjects that you would be able say "she's responsible" in.

The responsible student is what we usually call "self-motivated." She's interested in doing the work and knows that it feels good to do a good job. Her main motivation is doing well. She wants to make her parents proud, but that's not the main thing.

"It's nice when my parents tell me I've done a good job, but that's not the reason I do well," a student recently told me. "The main reason is that it feels good to do well. Plus, I don't have that worry on my shoulders about not doing well."

The Ups and Downs of the Responsible Student

There are a lot of good things happening when a student is being responsible. The biggest positive is that she is somewhat self-sufficient, depending on her age. Young students will still need quite a bit of guidance, even when they are responsible.

The only trap in dealing with the responsible student has more to do with the parents than anyone else.

Parenting the Responsible Student

There are two major things to keep in mind when it comes to the Responsible Student. First, she wants to know that you think she's doing a good job.

"You are doing a good job!"

Sometimes, we have a tendency to pay less attention to the child who is doing well in school. She isn't the squeaky wheel. She's the one we don't have to worry about. The risk of this is that the Responsible Student might end up feeling neglected.

The second issue, which is the trap, is that we tend to overparent the Responsible Student. Instead of being the Supporter, we drift into the Consultant role. This can make the Responsible Student feel like you don't trust her. Pulling back is a hard thing. But it is exactly what our kids need at times.

The Anxious Student

The Anxious Student looks a lot like the Responsible Student, at least from the outside. He does his work well, gets good grades, and completes his homework every day. But the Anxious Student doesn't feel so good about his performance. He has set very high standards and beats himself up if he doesn't meet them. He worries about the future quite a bit and he doesn't listen to facts that might calm him down. When told that he needs to go to bed since he has studied enough, he doesn't believe you.

The Ups and Downs of the Anxious Student

Anxiety can be a pretty good thing, if used in the right way. The Anxious Student tends to do good work. If a student forgets to study something, anxiety might be exactly what he needs to remember to study next time.

But it's not a happy place in the mind of an Anxious Student, especially for one who is generally anxious about a number of school subjects. His brain is often in the hyper-vigilant mode, keeping an eye out for any slip up. He tends to think either one of two thoughts when it comes to schoolwork:

1. If he performs exceptionally: "OK, I'm doing well, so I need to start thinking about the next assignment."

2. If he didn't perform exceptionally: "I am a horrible student. I'm an idiot. I need to study more and more and more."

Parenting the Anxious Student

Here are some do's and don'ts when it comes to helping the Anxious Student:

Do: Try to gently help them see that there could be other outcomes than the worst-case scenario. I say "gently" because if we are too abrupt or certain about our opinion, it will get dismissed quickly.

Don't: Tell them to "calm down." Although well meaning, this tends to be as effective as telling a baby to stop crying!

The Disorganized Student

"Did you pack your book bag?" you ask before bedtime. "Yep, it's all set," your son replies. Later that morning, he calls you from school and asks you to bring his math binder. "I thought you had packed it last night," you say. "Yeah, I guess I forgot."

If this sounds familiar, you know all about the Disorganized Student. This is the student who can never seem to find what he needs. You set up an organization system for him and, within a week, things are all over the place again. You always know when he has come home because of the trail of his shoes, book bag, papers, etc.

"He just needs a system," the organized parent will say. But every system seems to fall apart pretty quickly, which just increases the frustration of the parents, especially the more organized parent.

The Ups and Downs of the Disorganized Student

Yes, there are some good qualities of a Disorganized Student. Recent research on organized vs. disorganized people shows that disorganized people tend to enjoy life more! Not surprising, since they spend much more time enjoying themselves instead of organizing! But I think students who are very disorganized don't tend to enjoy life as much. For the organized person, when things are out of place, it creates stress and anxiety, which can only be reduced by organizing or tidying up. Then the brain begins to function normally again. For people who tend to be disorganized, their brain tolerance for clutter is much higher. Seeing things lying around doesn't produce the same biochemical reaction as it does for the organized student. When your Disorganized Student asks, "What's the big deal?" he really means it! It is not a big deal to him.

The bad news is that the *tendency* to be organized or disorganized is not much under control of the student. If you like being organized, it has probably been that way for quite a while, maybe all of your life. The "organization" tendency is an issue of how well our brains can tolerate chaos.

This is not to say that organization is set in stone. I am saying that the *tendency* is pretty much set in stone. For example, I am certain that my tendency is toward clutter, which wasn't a big deal growing up. But, since becoming an adult and marrying someone who is more neat and organized, I have learned how to become more organized. If, on a 1–10 scale, I was a 4 in high school, I am probably a 7 now. I have learned how to be more organized, but it will never come naturally.

Parenting the Disorganized Student

The Disorganized Student needs your help. He doesn't need you to do it for him, but he probably won't do it on his own. Being the Consultant is of great benefit to the Disorganized Student. Being the Boss only works when rewards are in order. Unfortunately, punishments don't help him become more organized.

The Unmotivated Student

"Don't you want to do better in school?" a mother asked Diana, her middle school daughter, during their first session with me. Diana, a 12-year-old 7th grader, looked like she had heard that question a million times. "No, Mom, I don't want to do better in school. What I really want is to drop out so I can live with you forever. I so enjoy these little chats we have. I would really miss them if I had to go to college and get a job and live as far away from you AS POSSIBLE!" I could tell I was going to enjoy working with her! Her sense of timing and sarcastic tone is so much better, to a family counselor, than the somewhat typical one-syllable answers we often get from middle schoolers.

Although Diana's verbal wit was out of the ordinary, her struggles with motivation were not so unusual. She was "underperforming," according to her teachers. She could do so much better. I asked her to complete this sentence: "Diana is so smart; I don't know why she doesn't try. She has so much _____." Diana quickly said: "Potential!" She continued, "Yes, I hear that all the time. It gets tedious very quickly."

Does Diana remind you of someone you know? If so, you've got a student dealing with motivation issues. She will answer all the probing questions correctly about wanting to do well in school, but when the rubber meets the road, the grades stay the same.

Ups and Downs of the Unmotivated Student

There is a reason why some students are unmotivated. It protects them. It protects them from disappointment. Their own disappointment with themselves. And the disappointment from others. They tell themselves: "Don't try too hard, you'll just disappoint yourself." This is mostly a coping mechanism. It is a way for them to feel OK about themselves. Why? Being lazy is better than being incompetent.

I firmly believe that unmotivated people are not born that way. It is something that happens as they deal with life and try to be successful.

Universally, children want to improve. Your daughter says, "Look at me!" when she is doing her first jump into the pool, and you praise her. She probably won't just settle for jumping in after that. At some point, this summer or maybe next summer, she'll want to dive in to the pool. It is her nature to want to improve and get better.

This desire to improve is not just within some of us, it is within all of us. We all like to rest on our laurels for a bit, but then the itch to succeed gets to us and we look for the next challenge. The Unmotivated Student has had the natural desire for success switched to "Low" for some reason. It could be that, after a few years of working really hard for OK grades, they just don't know how much more they can do.

Parenting the Unmotivated Student

The Unmotivated Student usually responds, albeit slowly, to the Supportive Parent. Although it seems counterintuitive, "going along" with the Unmotivated Student can sometimes help.

"I'll never get a good grade with Ms. Jennings," your daughter tells you. Instead of jumping to the expected and rejected comments like "That's not true. I'm sure you can get a good grade if you try harder," try "You're pretty sure it's not going to change, huh?"

Stop there. Don't add anything else! Sometimes, after a few comments like this, your child might then begin to play her own "devil's advocate" and begin looking at the other side of the problem.

The I Don't Care Student

The I Don't Care Student is a special challenge. He probably has moved into this stage after spending some time in the Unmotivated stage. His answer about wanting to do well is "I Don't Care." When asked what he wants to do when he grows up: "I Don't Care." Reminding him that if he doesn't do his homework, he won't get to see his friends on Friday, he responds: "So what? They were just going to do something boring anyway."

"I don't know," "I don't care," "Doesn't bother me"—these are the mantras of the I Don't Care Student. Every time you try to increase motivation, it backfires. Every attempt at praise is greeted with a lukewarm response, if any response at all. This is the Unmotivated Student on steroids.

I Don't Care Students don't usually start showing up until the beginning of middle school, when there have been so many unsuccessful challenges that it has worn away any desire to have a desire. Sometimes, when he does well on something, you will praise him and tell him what a good job he did and how proud you are. Then, sometimes the very next day, he will bring home an F on something very similar. This is especially confusing and aggravating. Why did he bring home an F when it was clear he could do better?

Ups and Downs of the I Don't Care Student

It is so much safer to say, "I don't care," than to say, "I care," and then screw up. This is the root issue for an IDCS. He has tried and not succeeded so many times, and dealt with so many challenges and disappointments, that he doesn't even *want* to try anymore. "Why should I care? I'll only screw it up," he might think. But he won't say that out loud. He will just repeat his favorite line: "I don't care."

The IDCS is in a fragile state, even though he looks like he cares about nothing. Don't believe what you see. Just like any other kid, the IDCS wants to succeed. But he is at a complete loss about how to do that.

Parenting the I Don't Care Student

The IDCS doesn't leave us many choices. Being supportive only creates more I Don't Care's. Giving advice never works because there is NO motivation. Which only leaves us the option of the Boss. The main thing to keep in mind is to not worry if he says: "I don't care if you take everything away." Just keep being the Boss.

The Defiant/Argumentative Student

There are two types of Defiant Students: the Sneaky Defiant and the In-Your-Face Defiant.

The Sneaky Defiant Student's goal is to get away with not doing work by deceit.

I recently worked with a student who is a master at this. While Todd was doing his homework, his father came in and asked, "Are you almost done with that?" "Yep, just finished," Todd said. Dad then said, "Great, let's go get some dinner."

In fact, though, he hadn't finished his homework. And when Dad found out, he was furious. "You lied to me! I asked if you were done with your homework, and you said yes." Todd replied, "You asked me if I was done with *that*. I thought you meant my math work. I was just finishing it. It all depends on what the meaning of 'that' is."

Nice try, Todd. But his dad saw right through it (just like you did!). Todd was trying to get away with not doing the homework by being deceptive. He knew exactly what his father meant. When I laughed and asked Todd, "Really, that's the best you could have done?" he sheepishly grinned and admitted he was just trying to get away with it.

The Sneaky Defiant Student "loses" things very easily. "I think I lost that note from the teacher. Let me look again." He "forgets" to stay after school. "Detention was today? I thought it was tomorrow." He "misunderstands" things quite often. "I thought you meant that I should call you if I was coming straight home, not if I went to McDonald's after school."

The Sneaky Defiant is usually not the first born; he has watched his older sibling be openly defiant and has seen how badly that goes. I remember watching my brother get into huge arguments with my father about homework. I quickly learned to tell him what he wanted to hear, in hopes that he wouldn't follow up!

The In-Your-Face Defiant Student is just what it sounds like. The defiance happens right in your face. There is nothing sneaky about it. I remember, when growing up, my brother and I defied our parents very differently. My brother would tell my parents "no" right to their faces. I would say yes and then not do it! Here are some examples of how the In Your Face Defiance looks:

- "No, I'm not doing it now. I'll do it later."
- "Leave me alone. I can do it myself!"
- "That's not the way my teacher taught me. Let me do it my way."

Ups and Downs of the Defiant Student

In some ways, the In-Your-Face Defiant Student has some really good characteristics. She usually has a very strong sense of self, and is strong enough to stand up and state what she thinks is right. She usually wants more independence and thinks she has earned it. Even if her assessment is wrong or her logic is faulty, she certainly has an opinion of what is right for her and she is not afraid to express it.

The problem, of course, is that she might often be wrong. She thinks she knows what is best for her, but she doesn't have the experience and wisdom to make the right decisions. To add fuel to the fire, the more you counteract with an In-Your-Face response, the worse it tends to get.

Both types of Defiant Student share the same inside thoughts:

"I think I know what's best, and I DO NOT want to have my parents call the shots. I will do it my way, or the highway. Even if I think that your way might be better, I won't do it because that you would make you think you were right."

Parenting the Defiant Student

The Defiant Student probably won't change by your being the Supportive Parent, or by being a Consultant. Being the calmest Boss around is the only way of influencing the Defiant Student. Your goal is to give them as little as possible to rebel against. Keep in mind Marlon Brando's answer to "What are you rebelling against?": "Whaddya got?"

Rules and consequences. Rules and consequences. Don't worry at first about whether the rules are working, because I guarantee you, they won't. But in time, they will.

The Blaming Student

"It's not my fault!" is the mantra of the Blaming Student. When you ask about the poor grade, the answer will be some combination of these responses:

- "He didn't go over any of that in class."
- "He's a horrible teacher."
- "He treats all the boys unfairly."
- "He hates me. He's always telling me to shut up."
- "Nobody got a good grade."
- "I was sick that day."

If those don't tend to have the desired effect, he will then turn the blame on you:

- "You expect too much."
- "Why do you think it's always my fault?"
- "You never believe me."
- "If you would back off, I could do better."

These all have the same basic message: "It's not my fault. It's someone else's fault."

Ups and Downs of the Blaming Student

The blaming student often has a very fragile sense of confidence. Call it "self-esteem" or "self-image." It all tends to mean the same thing: He doesn't think he is strong enough to handle saying, "Maybe it's my fault." So he will go to great lengths to convince you (and himself) that it is someone else's fault. That's why, when you try harder to convince him of his responsibility, he becomes even more blaming. He can't handle the truth, so he will make up another reality, one he can handle better.

Parenting the Blaming Student

The biggest thing to keep in mind when it comes to the Blaming Student is this:

Don't get into conversations with the goal of trying to make the student shift the blame to himself.

When you spend your energy trying to stop the "It's someone else's fault" comments, you are wasting your time. Kids who have moved into the blame game are not going to shift from their position very easily. Instead of focusing on who is to blame, focus on the reality of the situation. For example, imagine that your student came home with a bad grade on a test. He immediately tells you that it was unfair; the teacher didn't teach half of the stuff on the test.

Instead of saying something like "I'm sure he taught it. You probably weren't listening," consider saying something like "Well, what are you going to do? That bad grade is going to make it harder to improve your final grade in the class. Any ideas?"

The first comment, although probably true, will just elicit an argument. The Blaming Student is not going to say, "Maybe you're right—I should pay more attention!"

The second comment, though, avoids the blame game completely and focuses on the future. I have seen this work well a number of times when dealing with a Blaming Student.

The Truths vs. the Myths about Kids

"Kids these days…"

It didn't take that long for us to start sounding like our parents, did it? When I was young, "Kids these days…" was something I heard from old men talking about how irresponsible the youth were. Now, we're saying the same thing about the next generation! Let's look at some of these things we say. Some of them are myths, some are true sometimes, and some are right on target.

"Kids these days...are lazy."

I was recently working with a mom, a dad, and their teenage son. The main issue was motivation. He was getting C's and D's in school, and the parents were stumped about what was going on.

"He doesn't have ADHD, he isn't depressed, and we've drug-tested him," his mom said.

"I think he's just lazy," his dad added. He then asked his son, "Why don't you do better in school?"

As Dad was asking this question, I could see a little smirk begin to develop on their son's face. He paused for just the right amount of time and said, "Because I'm lazy?"

I quickly found out that their son was anything but lazy. He had a ton of friends and spent a good deal of time with them. He was funny and was often planning things to do on the weekends. He loved snowboarding and spent as much time as he could on the slopes. This was not a lazy kid.

But something was getting in the way of him being more successful in school. I could definitely rule out laziness as one of the factors. The problem with labeling kids as "lazy" is that it doesn't help us figure out what we can do to help. It's a bit like the car mechanic saying, "Your car doesn't work." It states something, but doesn't help figure out how to make it better.

Try this...

The student who we might label "lazy" is probably one or two of the student types described earlier in the chapter. He is definitely unmotivated about some or all of his schoolwork. "He's unmotivated about history," is a much more specific statement. It's a statement we can work with.

When you start thinking, "He's lazy," try to stop yourself. Instead, ask, "Why would he be so unmotivated about his schoolwork when he can be so motivated about other areas of his life?"

"Kids these days...don't realize how good they have it."

I agree. They don't realize how good they have it. Since they might not have experienced tough times yet, they really have no reference point about how good it is for them. As you will read later in the book, I was one of those kids who didn't realize how good I had it, and that was a constant source of argument between me and my parents.

In all likelihood, I would guess that your life has been more difficult than your kids' lives. They probably have more opportunities, have played more sports and possibly even an instrument or two. They have more things and more ways to entertain themselves than we could have possibly imagined when we were kids 25 or 40 years ago. The problem is that we often expect gratitude from them, when they aren't really sure why they should be grateful, since they don't have a frame of reference about how good they have it. If they're not grateful, we think, then they should at least get good grades or something.

I suppose I can't really call this one a myth, since it's probably true that they don't realize how good they've got it. I don't think this is a bad thing, actually. It means we are doing what we are supposed to be doing: providing a good home for our children and hopefully giving them better opportunities than we had.

Try this...

Instead of saying, "He doesn't know how good he's got it," while rolling your eyes, try this instead: "Thank goodness he has no idea how good he has it. Thank goodness he hasn't had to experience violence, hunger, a lack of clothing, poor shelter, an addicted parent. Thank goodness I have provided a childhood where these things are not a part of his day-to-day life." There are other ways to engender gratitude. Spend some time as a family volunteering with those who are struggling. It won't take long for most kids to understand how lucky they have it.

"Kids these days...don't take responsibility."

Raise your hand if you agree with this one! This is a big issue for many parents. There are definitely some values that all parents share, and this is one of them. I have not met a parent yet who would like a child to be irresponsible! It's something we all strive for. If that's the case, why are we struggling with instilling responsibility so much?

I would agree that irresponsibility in kids is probably a truth , at least to a certain extent. There is a wave of kids these days who are not interested in taking responsibility for their schoolwork. This book will help you turn the tide in the other direction.

One of the most important, and most difficult, jobs as a parent is to engender a desire for success in our children. We cannot *make* our children responsible. *Making* a kid more responsible is a contradiction in terms. Responsibility, true responsibility, needs to come from within the student. But that doesn't mean we are powerless. We can, and we should, be powerful agents in increasing responsibility. Keep reading to see how to do it.

"Kids these days...aren't creative."

I recently read a *Newsweek* article[2] about the declining creativity in America's youth. In summary, the article describes that creativity, as measured by an assessment tool developed in 1958, is declining in today's children. The article then blames the usual suspects: TV, video games, the Internet, and... you guessed it: schools.

I've got a significantly different take on "kids these days" and sometimes feel like I'm in the significant minority. First, let me tell you why I'm so optimistic about our youth.

I am a licensed professional counselor in private practice in Reston, Virginia, which is a suburb of Washington, DC. I specialize in working with children and teens dealing with difficulties: school issues, underachievement, behavior problems, depression, etc. I have the privilege of talking with kids about their lives, feelings, ideas, and dreams for about five hours of my workday. It's an amazing job, and I'm amazed at how few people get to spend so much time just talking with kids. The kids I work with tell me pretty regularly that they have never had someone sit and talk with them for an hour and just be interested in their lives, their feelings, and their ideas.

Because of this privilege, I think I have a good idea of what's happening with kids these days. At least the kids in my little section of the world. And I have to say that I am impressed and amazed, sometimes to the point of being stunned.

I am impressed at their ability to think through ideas and synthesize new ways of considering things. I have watched as kids make amazing leaps of logic and not know exactly how they got there. Kids in the last ten years have been living such a radically different existence than any other generation before them, which our ways of measuring their progress don't work.

One last word about creativity. Remember the study I mentioned? The one that used a test developed in 1958 to measure creativity? I think the problem is that we are using a creativity measurement that is 50 years old! I think it's time we developed newer creativity measures!

Try this...

Try to begin considering your child's creativity differently. Our worlds have become so different from our children's worlds that it is sometimes hard to see the ways they are being creative. Spending ten minutes watching my kids play an online strategy game together is a quick reassurance for me that their creativity and problem-solving abilities are developing just fine!

Don't Freak Out Summary

- Our kids' styles will give us great insight about how they are feeling and what they need at any given moment. We need to just have patience to pay attention and respond appropriately without freaking out.

- Our kids' styles will fluctuate. As they do, we need to adjustment our approaches. As no child is expected to be consistently perfect, no single parenting style will work universally.

- Freaking out never works. It is, at best, a short-term solution to subdue the momentary symptom without addressing the root problem.

Don't Freak Out Exercise

Take a minute and think about the myths that might get in the way of you helping your child. Rank yourself on a 1-5 scale for each myth you think might get in the way of being the best leader possible.

... has my genes.	1 2 3 4 5
...don't realize how good they have it.	1 2 3 4 5
...don't take responsibility.	1 2 3 4 5
...aren't creative.	1 2 3 4 5
...are lazy.	1 2 3 4 5

Now, write down what you can tell yourself next time you think this myth is getting in the way.

_____

_____

CHAPTER FOUR

Understanding the Pressures of Parenting

Having a child is easy. Becoming a good parent is hard. And like any job, the quality of our performance reflects how much we put into it, how quickly we learn, and how willing we are to adapt. With all due respect to previous generations, parenting today is just more challenging.

Though today's children face the same universal challenges as their predecessors—peer pressure, parental expectation, violence, substances, etc.—there are several basic differences that make parenting today so difficult. Although this is not intended to become a lecture on why we have it so much tougher, identifying why things are different and more challenging will lay the foundation for successfully conquering the trials we face.

First, everything today is accelerated, more information-driven than experience gathered, and infinitely more accessible. Now I may not be young, but I'm not the old guy sitting on the park bench yelling at the kids on their Razor scooters to slow down. Twenty-five or 40 years ago, our parents simply did not have to worry about the Internet, cyber predators, the level of violence shown on network TV, the availability of synthetic drugs, and so on.

Second, we are the bridge generation to the Information Age. But we were not raised in it. And, for most of us, it is a foreign language. So we constantly have to play catch up and educate ourselves while our kids are flying in front. This means that the one piece of the puzzle we have always been able to stake claim to with indisputable confidence—experience—is not at our disposal.

Third, the expectation of the role of "parent" has completely transformed. When we were kids, the norm was that our fathers were the primary earners and our mothers were the primary caregivers and homemakers. It was unusual for the mother to work and, if she did, it almost never interfered with running the house. Fathers rarely coached their kids' teams, would never come to soccer practice at 3 P.M., and certainly were not responsible for many of the errands, tasks, and duties of running a household.

While these three major areas offer a global view of the new challenges faced by today's parents, they simply magnify longstanding challenges we face as parents—especially when it comes to schooling our kids.

Let's take a look at the pressures we face as parents and how we can best overcome them:

Pressure #1: Peer Pressure

I am not talking about the peer pressure that our kids experience. I am talking about parent peer pressure. Yes, parent peer pressure.

I think mothers in particular suffer from this. What I have seen over and over again is that most mothers tend to compare themselves with those other moms who are functioning in the 99.9 percentile—or at least appear to be. I recently read a mothers magazine that profiles local moms. The article went something like this:

"Susie is the mother of six children and works a full-time job as the executive director of a local nonprofit. She is very involved in her church and volunteers to bring meals to the elderly. Halloween is her favorite holiday because she makes each child's elaborate costume by hand. She also bakes from scratch all the goodies for her children's school." And on and on...

I am not making this up. The magazine features profile after profile of these "Moms on Steroids" who are being highlighted as role models.

I would love to hear one of the profile interviews go something like this:

Journalist: How do you do it all?

Mother: Well, it was tough at first, but I eventually developed a system. First I found that I didn't really need seven, or even six hours of sleep. I can do pretty well on about four. Then, I eliminated all of the things I used to do for me, such as working out, going to the doctor, reading, eating healthy meals, etc. When I finally focused on the fact that my kids come first, it wasn't too hard.

What kind of role model are we highlighting? Don't take care of you— just take care of everyone else.

I feel a bit presumptuous talking about this issue, since, clearly, I am not a mother. But I am concerned that these are the type of women we are putting on a pedestal for everyone else to emulate.

This idea reminds me of a real mother who shared with me her story about losing, and eventually regaining, her identity. Her name is Hillary. Hillary's story is one that, I think, many mothers can relate to.

When you first meet Hillary Tattersall, your initial impression is of the epitome of the 40-something, high-level executive. Tall, attractive, and outgoing; yet she doesn't take over the room. When you talk with her, you feel like she genuinely cares about what you are saying.

"I was the first generation of women that were expected to be professionals. Get good grades, get into a good college, so that you can be a great professional. All the focus was to be a professional. That's all I was trained for. I never played (or even wanted to play) school or house as a kid. I played office.

"For years I was an executive for a national charitable foundation. It was a very stressful, very high- energy position. I honed some skills that I found very hard to let go of later. I was driven, I expected perfection from those around me, and I was impatient. Impatient people are rewarded in sales. It was around the time that my kids were just moving into elementary school that my husband I and decided that I would leave my career and be a full-time mom.

I think many families can relate to the Tattersalls. You get to a point where you would like someone to be at home with the kids, so you make the leap into becoming a one-income family. We do it for our kids, in hopes that this will be best for everyone.

Hillary continued: "It didn't take long to realize that the skills I learned in the business world were not going to work at home. All of the sudden, I'm taking 20 minutes to tie a pair of shoes, and it was beginning to drive me nuts! I was the first generation of women to be trained and rewarded for impatience, and then I come home and realize patience is the biggest skill I need to be a good mom.

"I went from living my high-speed life on the autobahn, to putting along on a country lane. I began a mantra that helped me through at first, but it really began wearing on me: 'You are doing it for the children. Be selfless, be selfless, be selfless.'

"My patience really took a hit when I began to sit at the kitchen table helping my kids with their homework. I would rather watch paint dry, than have to sit there with them during homework time. How can I run a million-dollar golf tournament, and not have the patience to help my children read? I was supposed to help him, but I was sitting there tapping my foot, doing my laundry list, and slowly going nuts."

What happened to Hillary? She accepted the myth that, when we become parents we lose our own identity and focus completely on the kids. Especially because she had left a full-time career, she felt that pressure even more. Add to that the fact she felt woefully unprepared for the challenge, made it much more difficult for her to feel anything but pressure, pressure, pressure.

How to Conquer Parental Peer Pressure

What do we tell our kids about peer pressure? "If your friend jumped off the house, would you do it too?" (And by the way, after looking at the number of YouTube videos of kids jumping off houses, I'm afraid the answer to this question, from many kids, would be…"Yes!")

If we challenge our kids to not give in to peer pressure, it's important that we don't, either. It requires us to stay concentrated on "why" we are doing something and checking to make sure it is *not* related to showing others that we are a good parent.

In truth, we are only trying to convince ourselves that we are a good parent. The problem is, there is only one person who can accurately measure our performance: ourselves. Comparing myself to others will either make me feel better, or worse. It just depends on which dad I'm comparing.

I think it is very important that we reign in our parenting peer pressures. We will go crazy with anxiety and stress if we try to keep up with the neighbors, and our kids will end up burning out.

Pressure #2: Time Pressure

This is the pressure to duplicate yourself so you can attend all activities and functions. It is the pressure you feel when there are not enough hours in the day. This is a huge problem for many parents. The problem with most study tips for parents is that they take a lot of time.

Try this experiment: Google a search similar to "Homework tips for parents," look at some of the top websites, and read their suggestions. When I did this, two things popped up right away:

One: Many of the tips are outdated, misinformed, and/or ineffective. I will address this issue in Chapter 11.

Two: Almost every suggestion requires a significant amount of time commitment from the parents. We have gone, in one generation, from a culture where parents rarely checked homework, to one where parents are expected to be involved in every homework session. The scheduling demands of this expectation is hitting families, especially mothers, smack dab in the middle of our most precious resource: time.

So, what tends to happen is that we quickly try a new approach to homework, but something else ends up getting neglected. Guess what that tends to be? Ourselves. And the less we take care of ourselves, the less helpful we are going to be for our kids. The time pressure is huge for modern families.

How to Conquer Time Pressure

One of the really great ways me and my family keep track of our schedules is by using Google Calendar. We each have a separate color for each person, and we put in new activities as we schedule them. Work hours, practice times, parties, trips, graduations, etc., all get put into the calendar. Both of our kids have access to the calendar as well. When they ask about an event, or what time the game is this weekend, we can just tell them to check the online calendar.

I recently reviewed a typical week and was stunned at how little white space is left. Even though we are vigilant about keeping our time commitments to a reasonable level, the pressure of time is always on us. This recent Christmas, as I was working on finishing the manuscript for this book, I asked my daughter what she wanted for Christmas. "Time," was her answer. "Time to sit and watch movies together. Time to just spend as a family." In this day and age, when we assume that all that kids want is just more stuff, the biggest thing my daughter wanted from me was my time.

Try this activity. Take your typical weekday and schedule out, in 60-minute increments, what the day looks like:

Time	Activity	Time	Activity
5 a.m.		4 p.m.	
6 a.m.		5 p.m.	
7 a.m.		6 p.m.	
8 a.m.		7 p.m.	
9 a.m.		8 p.m.	
10 a.m.		9 p.m.	
11 a.m.		10 p.m.	
12 p.m.		11 p.m.	
1 p.m.		12 p.m.	
2 p.m.		1 a.m.	
3 p.m.		2 a.m.	

If you see a good amount of blank blocks, that's a positive sign. If you have some sections dedicated directly to yourself (such as gym, coffee with friends, etc.), even better. But if the "me" time has gone by the wayside, it might be time to consider readjusting things for the sake of yourself and your family.

I know for a fact that when I take care of myself, both physically and mentally, I am a much better father. When I don't take care of myself, I am not nearly as pleasant to be around.

Pressure #3: Two-Earner Pressure

The time pressure of the family with two parents who both work full-time jobs adds another very difficult pressure. Now, the time needed to be with the kids is even more compressed with all of the other day-to-day activities that can't be taken care of during the workday. Shopping, cooking, bill paying, arguing with the insurance company, etc., are all compressed into the few hours after work. Add to that all of the child-centered activities, like homework, chores, etc., and the time issue is magnified tremendously.

There are a number of benefits to two-earner households, along with a number of trade-offs for those benefits. Unfortunately, many families do not find a way to maximize the benefits and reduce the trade-offs.

How to Conquer Two-Earner Pressure

How can you deal differently with time so that it no longer rules you? Here are some suggestions to consider.

1. Allocate funds to maximize the benefit year round:

I recently worked with a family that came up with a method for dealing with the time issue in a very unique and effective way. In the father's words:

"We figured out that we were in this time trap that none of us liked. The trap was this: both of us worked full time, which is great because it gives us the chance to live in a neighborhood with a really good public school, and the kids love their neighbor friends. Having two incomes also gave us an extra amount to go on a couple of really nice vacations during the year. But the problem was that, by the time the vacation came, we were all so burned out and cranky that no one ended up having a good time. Instead of being able to sit back and enjoy ourselves, we were just as irritated and tired as usual—just at the beach or in a hotel.

"Here's what we decided to do: We totaled up the amount of money that we would spend on vacations each year and divided that number by 12 to see how much money there was for each month if we didn't go on vacation. Then my wife and I asked ourselves: If we were to use this money to hire someone to do the time-consuming, unpleasant things in our day-to-day or week-to-week lives, what would that be and how much would it cost?

"I hate cutting the grass," he said. "It's the last thing I want to do on the weekends. I'm cranky until I get it done and I'm cranky after it's completed.

So getting someone to cut the grass is on the top of the list. For my wife, it's cleaning the house. She said if she knew that someone would clean the house from top to bottom every other week, that would be a huge time and emotional load off.

"When we did the math we realized that, for less than the cost of our vacations, we could have these time- and energy-sucking things out of our lives for the whole year. It was a no-brainer for us. The kids weren't thrilled at losing the vacation time, but we have replace them with smaller day trips. I think the fact that their parents are happier year round more than makes up for the difference."

I love this story. Because it takes a problem that so many families deal with and finds a solution that might not be obvious. Free up your time on a day-to-day basis instead of saving all year and trying to fit some rest and relaxation into a few days.

I understand that many of us don't have the extra money to go on vacations, let alone hire someone to do our lawns, but by looking at the way we use our time and our money and by being creative, there might be ways to free up some time.

2.   Make adjustments on time burners:

Time burners are those things we do that burn time and get us away from what we want to do. Cooking, cleaning, laundry, grocery shopping, yard work, etc.—these are things that have to get done, but don't really add any value to the family relationship. I have yet to hear a child say, "Gee, Mom, I really enjoyed our time together scrubbing toilets!"

I am suggesting that you take a hard look at how you are spending your time and see if adjustments can be made without significantly affecting your family. Take dinner, for instance.

Let me be clear about this point. I think homemade meals are fantastic. I was raised by an excellent cook, who taught me a great many things about cooking well. I love to cook, especially from scratch. But there are many,

many times when I need to "scrap the scratch" idea because I just don't have the time. I am going to take a risk at being kicked out of the parenting professionals club by suggesting the heretical idea that it's OK (even great) to save time by cooking less.

Most of us don't cook a lot anyway. And we feel guilty about that. I'm asking you to remove the guilt; tell yourself it's OK to spend less time cooking so you can spend more time with your kids, or even with yourself.

Does that mean pizza night every night? Maybe, but then you will end up feeling guilty (and rightly so) about not providing a healthy meal at least a few nights a week. It is difficult, but not impossible, to eat well and save tons of time. I recently had a discussion at a dinner party about the merits of mashed potatoes from scratch vs. the refrigerated, pre-mashed version (I'll admit I'm not the most interesting party guest). I would rather spend the extra 30 minutes with my kids helping them with a tough math concept than peeling, boiling, and mashing a starch product that would take 30 seconds to microwave. So I swallow my "made from scratch" pride and buy the thing that will give me 30 more minutes with my kids.

How about other time burners? I have heard many a dad tell me that, instead of buying the new mower when the old one went kaput, he hired a local college kid or a neighbor trying to make extra money to cut his grass. Think of the hours you could then have with your kids instead of spending that time on home upkeep.

Whether it is reallocating funds, adjusting how you take care of a task, or simply choosing one activity over another, there are plenty of ways to "create" a bit more time.

Pressure #4: Participation Pressure

Participation pressure is the stress we feel that we should participate in everything and have our child participate in everything.

This is a very self-imposed pressure. We can quickly feel stress that we are not doing everything we should for our kids. We feel that if we don't grab every opportunity, our children will suffer.

One day, we received a letter in the mail. It looked very important, with a thick envelope, embossed printing, a gold seal…the works. It was addressed to "The Parents of Maximilian McNerney." No one calls my son "Maximilian," so I was a little dubious. But it looked so fancy!

Max was invited to participate in a leadership program in Washington, DC. He was one of "only a few students" at his school to be selected. The letter goes on to tell us all the great leadership opportunities he will have, and how these formative years would determine how he will deal with high school and beyond.

I felt a number of feelings simultaneously. On one hand I was proud of my son and on the other hand I was worried about how we could afford this program. The letter anticipated my worry with "How much is your child's future worth?" OK, pour on the guilt!

I was dealing with a classic case of participation pressure. If I didn't have Max participate in this program, he would end up not feeling like a leader. The letter made it sound like I would be dooming my son to a life of submissive destitution if he did not participate—or at least that's how my parental pressure–filled mind interpreted it. The problem was that I got sucked in a bit and started questioning myself. Fortunately, I resisted this pressure, telling myself that since we live close to DC, we could do a good part of the program ourselves. The decision was made easy when I found out that many—very many—of Max's friends also received this letter! My cynicism cranked into high gear, and I wondered if this organization knew how much we, as parents, deal with these pressures.

Some pressures to participate are a bit less obvious: School performances, parent volunteering, after-school tutoring, sports, bake sales, fundraising, PTA. The list is endless.

How to Conquer Participation Pressure

When you are considering adding something to your family's schedule, ask yourself:

> The real costs of adding activities is more than just money

Specifically, how will this add to our children's (or my) quality of life?

Specifically, what will this cost me? What will it cost my children?

It is a good exercise to actually list out the reasons why we are adding a new activity, lesson, sport, skill, instrument, etc. In doing this exercise, be brutally honest with yourself about how it is going to add to you and your children's life. "I will feel great seeing my child playing Mozart during the piano recital," is, for most of us, a real factor in why we want something. Write it down.

Regarding the cost, be brutally honest.

What money will this cost?

How much time will it cost?

Time for the actual activity

Travel time

Time nagging the kids

How much aggravation will this cost?

I think if we did this exercise more often, our pressures about time and participation will decrease. This is why the pressure of time and the pressure of participation are so intricately connected. When we take a hard look at our participation pressures and make a realistic choice, it will alleviate much of our time pressures. Simultaneously, taking this objective look should alleviate guilt in the decision-making process.

Pressure #5: Teacher Pressure

Teacher pressure is that thing we feel when we get the e-mails saying, "Your son didn't turn in his homework again today. Please be sure that he does his homework and brings it to school." Or you are at the parent-teacher conference and are asked, "How can we work together to make sure your daughter completes her homework?" Even though the teacher says, "work together," you know the real message: "Get it together."

Teachers can have a lot of power in how students feel, but they also have a ton of influence on our feelings as well. We are insecure about this education thing. We sit at the parent-teacher conference and nervously wonder: "How are we doing?" We know it's not about us, but our emotions don't know that. And for some of us, are egos are also on the line.

How to Conquer Teacher Pressure

Remember: The teacher is your partner. Regardless of what she says, or implies, she is on the same team. You are all working toward your student's success. It would be nice

> Nothing good ever comes from trying to figure out who is to blame.

if all teachers dealt with parents effectively, but we are not there yet. If you are feeling that you are being blamed, don't accept it. Nothing good ever comes from trying to figure out who is to blame (see Chapter 1). The best approach is to plan what each person can do in the future that might produce some change. Identify each person's role in the partnership, and keep an open line of communication.

Pressure #6: Student Pressure

Students are feeling a great deal of pressure when it comes to schoolwork. I have spoken with kids as young as 8 who have told me that if they don't get straight A's, they won't go to Harvard—and they probably won't get a good job. Although most kids don't feel that strongly, the pressure that kids feel to perform is incredibly high. Where does this pressure come from? The main pressure generators are teachers, peers, and parents.

As with most difficult things in life, pressure is a good thing—to a point. I have seen so many kids who have let the pressure control them instead of them controlling the pressure, with very sad results. Kids convincing their parents to do things they never thought they would do, like letting kids stay up past (or way past) their bedtime to finish homework. Why is it OK to stay up late and ruin our sleep cycles for studying, but not for watching Monday Night Football?

How to Conquer Student Pressure

My daughter had a pretty difficult 5th grade year. She has always been a good, hard-working student, and her grades reflected it. In our school district, students move to middle school in 6th grade. So 5th grade would be her last year in elementary school. It was the intention of the 5th grade teacher to make sure all kids were ready for middle school, so the intensity and pressure was notched up quite a bit.

Shannon's feelings of pressure, of doing well, were very high. She began spending much more time on homework than we felt was good for her. I felt a lot of pressure to let her continue to focus so much energy on school. But I worried about her. I worried that her life was becoming singularly focused on school. I didn't want to give in to this pressure, but at the same time, I also wanted her to do well in school. But this much pressure in 5th grade?

As mentioned earlier, dealing with the Anxious Student is tough. Telling Shannon to "calm down" just made it worse. We eventually had to come to a couple of realizations:

1. Shannon's pressures were *her* pressures. They weren't ours. Regardless of how hard it was to say this, it was true. But this subtle nuance allowed us to pull back a bit and not try to solve the problem ourselves and rescue her.
2. We couldn't just convince her to "take it easy." Her self-imposed stresses were much more powerful than our advice and something

she needed to work through.

3. The only thing we could do was to put boundaries on the homework issue. Bed at the usual time, dinner with the family, plenty of play time and sports, etc.

Eventually, Shannon began to feel much better about 5th grade, and her worries decreased. Did we help her with it? Probably. But she did the lion's share of learning how to calm her own emotions.

Let me end this chapter by saying that I don't think pressure, on its own, is a bad thing. To expect a life with little to no pressure is just not possible. Pressure itself is actually not the problem. It is the amount of pressure we put on ourselves unnecessarily, and how we deal with pressure, that causes the problems.

Don't Freak Out Summary

- Although we talk a lot about the pressures kids feel, it is important to remember your own pressures.
- There are things you can do to decrease the parental pressures you are feeling. Consider trying one of the suggestions mentioned in the chapter.

Don't Freak Out Exercise

Think about each of these pressures and circle the number from 1-10 to indicate the level of pressure you feel. For example, the number 1 would be no pressure, all the way up to 10, the most pressure you could imagine.

	Not at all		Sort of		Pretty much		A Lot			Imagine the time!
Peer Pressure	1	2	3	4	5	6	7	8	9	10
Two-Earner	1	2	3	4	5	6	7	8	9	10
Participation	1	2	3	4	5	6	7	8	9	10
Teacher	1	2	3	4	5	6	7	8	9	10
Student	1	2	3	4	5	6	7	8	9	10

How do your circles look? Do you have many that are "5's" and above? That's a sure sign that you are over-pressured. Now take the same list and circle the pressures you think you can decrease. Lastly, write down a few sentences about what you can do to decrease this pressure:

_____

_____

Don't Freak Out Resource

For an online quiz on parental pressures, go to www.reducehomeworkstress.com/exercises/parent-pressure

CHAPTER FIVE

Applying the Homework Leadership Styles that Work

There are many parenting leadership styles we can use to help our kids with schoolwork. But often we don't know which one to use, and tend to pick a style based on our worry level at the time, rather than what our kids are demonstrating they need. In this chapter I will outline three different types of parenting leadership styles, help you determine when each would be appropriate, and share with you ways to interpret the signs kids give us.

The three leadership types to consider using are: The Supporter/The Fan, The Consultant, and The Boss.

The Supporter/ The Fan

The Supporter is a leader whose main goal is to support the activities of the student through encouragement, listening, and observing. As a Supporter, you understand that the best way you can increase school success is through encouragement. Either your student is doing well enough, or you know it wouldn't be helpful to use another approach because of your child's ambition and sense of responsibility about self-improvement.

At first glance, you might think this approach is the least powerful, but my experience is that this approach can be very powerful if used in the right situation. It sends a very strong message to your child:

"I have confidence in you."

"I believe you can do this."

"I'm impressed with you."

As the Supporter, your biggest tools are observation, listening, and reflecting.

Observing and Summing Up

I love the way that the book *How To Talk So Kids Will Listen* deals with the issue of observation. By observing, all we are doing is describing what we see, and then, if appropriate, summing it up in a word.

1. What do you see?

2. Sum it up in a word.

Let me offer a scenario and three ways you could use observation. You child has completed her homework, put her bag next to the door, and packed her lunch for the following day.

1. "I see you've got all your homework done, your bag is packed and by the door, and your lunch is packed."

2. "I see you've got all your homework done, your bag is packed and by the door, and your lunch is packed. That's what I call prepared."

Impressed vs. Proud

Something I have learned is how much more powerful the comment "I'm Impressed" can be compared to the comment "I'm Proud." When we say, "I'm Proud," we are saying one of these two things:

1. I am taking at least some credit for the accomplishment. "I'm proud we got that done."

2. Or we are saying something like "I'm proud to be called your parent."

My son and I were at a coffee shop, and a colleague I hadn't seen for years stopped by to say hello. When I told her what I had been up to for the past decade, she said, "Wow, Neil, I am really proud of you!" I thanked her, and we talked a bit longer and then said our goodbyes. Afterward, my son asked, "Why did she say she was proud of you? Was she your teacher? Did she help you?" I told him she wasn't my teacher but someone I had worked with ten years ago. He paused and said, "So she meant that she was impressed then, right?" My son intuitively knew the difference between the two terms.

Saying "I'm impressed" can be a much more powerful motivator than "I'm proud." Kids want to know their parents are impressed by them—and they want to take the credit for it! In fact it's good that they take the credit for it. It lets them know that their hard work is paying off. So next time you find yourself saying, "I'm proud," try switching it to "I'm impressed" and see how it works.

Hit and Run Praise

This is another one of those simple techniques that, if used well, can be very powerful. Hit and Run Praise means pretty much just that. You praise your child, using the suggestions above, and then get out of there before it gets screwed up! As parents, it can be hard to stop ourselves from giving advice, tweaking things a bit, and fine-tuning. But sometimes those extras are the very things that spoil the soup.

Example:

You daughter has been struggling with a certain subject, getting C's and D's on quizzes. Today, she comes home with a B! She's excited. So are you!

You say, "Great job! I'm really impressed!"

So far, so good, right? But you know what comes next…

You add, "Now why couldn't you have gotten B's on the other ones?"

Or

"So let's figure out how you can get an A next time."

Or

"I hope you can keep this up for the next quiz."

These additions can take away all of the good feelings that were happening up until then. Let's use an example from the working world. After a great presentation, your boss says, "Great job. Now why can't you present that well every time?" or "Let's look at what you can do to make it better next time." Do you feel the wind being sucked right out of your sails? Instead, think about how it would it feel if your boss just said, "Great Job."

Hit and Run Praise:

Describe what you see

Sum it up in a word

Get out!

To conclude, the Supporter is just supporting. You are trying to show the good progress your child is making and giving him a chance to evaluate himself. You are connecting with him and sharing in his progress without taking credit. You are setting your own ego, and your worries, aside and letting your child recognize and savor his accomplishments. The better we become at being the Supporter, the more likely our kids will stand on their own.

The Consultant

The Consultant is more active than the Supporter. When your role is the Consultant, you are still being the Supporter, plus you are adding information and advice when you think it will be received openly.

The art of being the Consultant is always in the delivery. Generally, success with this leadership style is based on how well the parent can deliver the message so that it will be heard. Anyone can tell someone what's wrong. That's easy. The hard part is telling someone what's wrong in such a way that they will actually listen, and maybe make some changes. That's the goal of the Consultant parenting leadership style: to deliver the advice in such a way so that it might actually be received and used!

Be Tentative

The greatest skill of the Consultant is learning how to speak tentatively. I remember a story I heard from Bill O'Hanlon, who is one of the pre-eminent change theorists in the field of family therapy. When Bill asked a father of five boys what his secret to parenting was, the father replied:

> "Raising kids is like watching each one of them jump onto a motorcycle, get it up to full speed, and ram right into a brick wall."

Not exactly an uplifting image, but I think we all can agree that being a parent sometimes feels that way, especially as they get older and sometimes make poor, even dangerous, decisions. But that's not the important part of the story.

The father continued:

> "The first kid, I didn't even know what was happening. Surely he isn't going slam into that wall. I was in denial. By the second kid, I knew what was ahead and screamed at him to stop. 'Don't you know what's going to happen if you keep going that way?!' But it didn't do any good. It wasn't until the last couple of kids that I began to understand what I needed to say was this: 'Now I'm not exactly sure, but I have a hunch that if you keep going the way you are, at the speed you are, you might end up crashing into that brick wall. But I'm not certain.' It was these kids that actually listened to me. They sometimes still crashed into that wall, but not nearly as often as the first few kids."

Please keep in mind I'm using this analogy for school-related issues. If you kid was really doing something dangerous, I wouldn't suggest the Consultant role.

The genius of being tentative lies in the fact that it allows the kid to save face. It allows the advice to be his decision, instead of it being your decision. It's amazing how many times kids will do the opposite of the advice given, just to prove they have a mind of their own. Will your kids still make mistakes? Sure. But being tentative will slow things down quite a bit before hitting that wall. Plus, your relationship will be intact so that you can help them out.

Put yourself in their place for a moment, using an adult scenario again. Suppose you are in a meeting with your supervisor. You are planning a presentation that you have to do together. Your boss would like it to be a lecture presentation with a question/answer period at the end. You think it would be better to have some audience interaction during the presentation, such as breaking into small groups.

Your boss says, "I know these people better than you. They are engineers and they hate small group participation. They just want the information so they can get back to work. Small group stuff never works with them."

How do you feel? Ignored? Angry? Unimportant? Stupid? Frustrated?

What is your opinion of your boss at that moment? He's dismissive, arrogant, a jerk? In this situation, I might be thinking, "Even if he's right, I'd like to prove him wrong since he thinks he's such a know-it-all. Why did he want me along if he's just going to tell me what to do and not listen to my ideas?"

Now, since he's your boss, you probably won't defy him. If you do, you might lose your job. But your opinion of him has decreased, and the relationship is strained. You probably won't bring up any new ideas out of fear they will be immediately rejected.

These are the same things our kids often feel about direct advice. The difference? They know we can't fire them. And their sense of independence will lead them to defy us—just to show us who's in charge.

A refrain I hear from many parents is: "If they would just do what I told them to do, their life would be so much easier. They would have better grades, more free time, and we would get along so much better."

This is all probably true. But from a kid's perspective, if they did it the way you told them, then they wouldn't be a human, they would be a robot. Some children's desire for being an independent person is so strong that they do things that are clearly harmful. But for them, the harm is less important than the desire to be their own person. So remember: Be tentative. Let your ideas become their ideas. Simply plant the seed.

Success Story

I had a recent example with my 5th-grade daughter. She was in the midst of a week of five quizzes and tests, and she was not happy. But she did feel pretty confident about the material. When I noticed she wasn't studying, I asked her about it.

"I think I'm ready. I don't need to study," she told me.

The first thing I did, which was the hardest, was to pause and not say anything. I bet you could predict what I wanted to say: "Really? Let me quiz you to find out." Or "Well, I want to you study anyway. It never hurts to study a bit more." Or I could remind her of past history, maybe a time when she didn't study because she thought she was ready, and her test grade suffered.

During the pause, however, I decided to calmly think about what role would be best. I didn't think the Supporter role was right for this situation. Just saying, "Good luck, I know you'll do great," didn't seem right. And being the Boss and making her study more didn't seem right either; I didn't actually know whether she was prepared or not. So I decided to try the Consultant:

"OK. I'm glad you feel like you are ready. But I remember when your brother had the same teacher, and the tests were pretty tough then. It might be a good idea to spend a little more time studying, but it's up to you."

I was so hoping she would then sneak away and do some more studying, but she didn't. The next day comes and she takes the test. When I ask her how it went, she told me, "Not so good. It was harder than I thought."

It took incredible strength for me to just shut up at this point and let her keep talking. "I'm sorry to hear that," was all I said. Trust me, I wanted to say more. But then I added, "So what do you think?"

She looked at me and said, "I think I'll go study for tomorrow's test right now. He's harder than I thought."

Then she did something completely unexpected. She hugged me and said, "I love you, Dad," and went to her room to study. After I was able to recover and think about what had just happened, I realized that it was exactly the type of interaction we want from our kids. She knew exactly what my opinion of studying was, but I force it on her. Since I gave her the option to choose, it was *her* choice, not mine. I think I got the hug and the "I love you" because she felt I cared about her and was going to let her decide how to handle the situation. Did she follow my Consultant advice? No. Not this time. Did she crash into that wall? Maybe a little. But this type of interaction is going to have a long-term, positive impact.

Besides, when was the last time a bad grade on a quiz in 5th grade carried more weight than a teachable moment and an "I love you."

The Boss

The Boss is the style most of us often resort to when first challenged by a situation with our kids. I suggest that instead, this should be our last resort. This is the role we frequently think of when we think of being the parent. It's the one where we tell our kids what to do and let them know what might happen if they don't. It's an effective role, and one we need to have at the ready, but not immediately.

The big difference between the Boss and the other roles can be summed up in a single word: consequences. Although both the Supporter and the Consultant deal with consequences, they are natural consequences borne by the decisions we let our children make, such as bad grades, etc. The Boss's effectiveness lies in the ability to enforce logical, artificial consequences with the goal of changing behavior.

Although you may have used the Boss before, consider some suggestions that will make this role much more effective:

1. Stay calm. This is crucial. Keep in mind why getting angry doesn't work: If you use the Boss when you are angry, you will lose the chance to be persuasive. The goal is to have your child change behavior because it's in his best interest, not because it will calm you down.

2. Be clear about the choices. Consider your statement to be like a computer program with an IF-THEN statement. "*If* you finish your homework before 7 p.m., *then* you can watch TV tomorrow. *If* you haven't finished it, *then* you will not be able to watch TV tomorrow."

3. Add "It's your choice." I know, this seems odd and somehow like we are relinquishing power. But saying, "It's your choice" only admits to reality. It is *always* the child's choice. Saying "It's your choice" allows for saving face, instead of the child feeling forced to make a certain decision. If it becomes a battle of wills, it's pretty likely that everyone will lose. If you carefully lead the conversation, there is a good chance that your child will make the right decision. The added benefit is that your child will also have increased his personal responsibility…something we dearly desire in our kids!

4. Change the subject; leave the room; don't keep talking! You have said your piece, now get out of there! The chances of things turning sour are huge if you stay around and talk some more. The more talking you do when you are the Boss, the greater the chance that you will lose your temper (or your audience).

Example:

Your son has a big project due in two weeks. He has had two months to work on it. You have helped him set up a plan so that he gets a little bit done every week. The plan has collapsed; he hasn't followed through on the weekly goals and now is very far behind.

"Get off my back!" he tells you. "I can get it done in plenty of time. Why don't you ever believe me? I'm not an idiot, you know."

You pause and tell yourself that you aren't going to take the bait this time and are going to ignore, for the time being, the disrespect. You review the fact that you have tried being both the Supporter and the Consultant, but with little effect. So you calmly tell him, "You have a choice this afternoon. Either you work for two productive hours on the project or you will not go to the football game tonight. *If* you work on the project this afternoon for two hours, *then* you are free to go to the game. I will decide if the two hours have been productive. It's your choice. By the way, I'm making pizza for dinner. What toppings do you want?"

He says, "This is stupid. I hate your pizza anyway."

You then put that imaginary piece of duct tape across your mouth, and leave the room before you undo all of your good, calm leadership. Parents need to pick their battles.

Do you see each of the four elements at work here? You stayed calm (didn't react to the disrespect). You were clear about the choices (football game or stay home). You said, "It's your choice." (In fact, you said it twice.) And you changed the subject and got out of there. You didn't take the bait, even though he was again disrespectful. Good job! Now go try it in real life!

An Example of How Not to Do It:

Recently, I had an experience where I clearly used the wrong leadership style. My approach was completely based on my mood, not on the situation.

It was an autumn Sunday after a very tiring work week and a weekend that was overflowing with activities. I was looking forward to an afternoon of watching football with my 7th grade son. He had agreed to get all of his homework done by noon so he wouldn't have to do it after dinner. All was going well until about 9 p.m., when my son began to pull out his homework again and quietly begins working on it.

"I forgot about something I needed to complete for tomorrow," he told me when he saw me glaring at him. Immediately suspicious, I said, "You didn't forget, you just wanted to watch football instead of finishing your homework. No TV tomorrow." Then I stormed out of the room. And when I went to say goodnight to him, he ignored me.

What did I do wrong?

One of the main things I have learned about parenting is this: When I am feeling anger start to rise, I need to take a minute to think about what I'm feeling and then decide how to act. I didn't do that in this situation.

Had I paused, I should have asked myself:

- Is this a pattern for him?
- Did he really lie (which I'll never be able to prove), or did he really forget?

Instead, I let my anger tell me which leadership style to use. I went immediately to The Boss. Plus I became The Mean Boss, since I was taking it personally.

The answer to the first question (Is this a pattern?) was actually "No." Forgetting to do homework was not a pattern for Max. He usually remembers his work. The second question (in this case, it was an implied statement), "You are lying," is an issue that tends to cause more problems. Knowing that my son is generally honest, I should have assumed he wasn't lying.

So, based on calmly looking at the facts, I probably should have led by being the Supporter. My response should have looked something like:

"Sorry to hear you've got more work. I hope it doesn't take long. I hope you don't stay up too late."

If his behavior was beginning to be a pattern, I might want to lead as the Consultant, which would have looked like this:

"Sorry to hear you forgot this assignment. What do you think you can do so you don't forget things like this? Did you use your assignment book? Is there anything I can do to help?"

For the sake of the example, let's say this behavior it was definitely a pattern, and being a Supporter and a Consultant hadn't worked. Therefore I choose the Boss. But this time I try to be the Calm Boss:

"I've noticed a pattern with forgetfulness. For the next week I want you to show me your work, your assignment book, and the online homework page from your teachers. You need to do all of these things before turning on any electronics."

So my steps should have been:

1. Pause and calm down

2. Assess the situation

3. Choose a leader type

Your role might vary from subject to subject, or sometimes from week to week. Your mood doesn't determine the role you play. Your anxiety doesn't determine the role, either. By taking a calm, unemotional look at the situation, you will be able to decide which role is right for the situation.

The C.A.L.M. Method

While discussing these leadership roles with a parent, she said, "OK, I get it that some styles work better than others, but I need a visual to understand when it would be best to use each of the styles." Chapter 6 features a list of the best leadership styles to try based on the type of behavior your child is showing. This will give you a quick "Go To" guide to figure out which style works best for each situation.

Don't Freak Out Summary

Keep it simple. There are only three effective ways to lead our children: the Supporter, the Consultant, and the Boss. The complexity lies in figuring out when to use each type, and how to use the style so that it might work.

Don't Freak Out Exercise:

Think about a challenging school-related situation with your child and record it here:

_____

_____

Now, determine which style your child is showing and circle it. If there are two styles, double circle the most prevalent one (if needed, see Chapter 3, "Decoding Our Kids," for a quick refresher).

    The Responsible Student
    The Anxious Student
    The Disorganized Student
    The Unmotivated Student
    The I Don't Care Student
    The Defiant Student
    The Blaming Student

Now, write down what you think you might do in the situation you noted above that would make things worse (or at least not help at all):

_____

_____

Lastly, pick the leadership style you think would work best and write down exactly how you would go about using that style for the best results for you and your child.

Leadership style (circle): Supporter Consultant Boss

_____

_____

CHAPTER SIX

Putting it Together—The Four-Step C.A.L.M. Method

By now, you should be pretty well versed in what works and what doesn't work when it comes to parenting kids with regard to homework. You understand yourself as a leader, and you understand the pressures and difficulties kids face today. You now have a good idea of each style and when to use it.

C.A.L.M. is a simple acronym that will help you remember the steps involved in creating a successful tone for your student's achievement.

C - Stay Calm

The foundation of the method is remembering to stay calm—or at least doing your best to appear calm! As discussed in Chapter 1, the calmer we become, the easier it is for our kids to succeed.

A - Assess Your Child

Using Chapter 3 as a reference, figure out which coping style is being used by your student. This will help you get some objective data to assess the situation, instead of just relying on anxieties to make an assessment. Which style is prevalent?

Responsible	Anxious	Defiant
Disorganized	Unmotivated	I Don't Care
Blaming		

L - Pick a Leadership Style

Using Chapter 5 as a reference, figure out which leadership style would work best. Take some time to consider the pitfalls of each style as well. For example, if you have selected the Consultant role, try to stay a bit tentative.

Here's a cheat sheet on which leadership style to try first, not based on your worries but on what your child is doing:

The Student Role	First Try	Maybe Try	Never Try
The Responsible Student	Supporter	Consultant	Boss
The Anxious Student	Consultant	Supporter	Boss
The Disorganized Student	Consultant	Supporter	Punish Boss*
The Unmotivated Student	Supporter	Boss	
The I Don't Care Student	Boss	Supporter	
The Defiant Student	Boss	Supporter	
The Blaming Student	Supporter	Boss	

* Punishments tend to backfire more often with the disorganized student, whereas rewards tend to have a better outcome. Focus more on rewards with disorganized students instead punishments.

Be Persistent

I recently had a parent in my office who was working through these leadership styles and was able to determine that, based on her son's behaviors, she should be the Boss. She was feeling good about the whole process, until she asked, "So, how long until he changes his behavior?"

I paused for a moment, and then said, "One day longer than he estimates you will give up."

She laughed and said, "I was afraid you'd say that. He knows I'll try something and that I can get pretty impatient. Sometimes it seems like he's waiting me out!"

The biggest challenge, at this point, is holding the line—not giving up too soon. The "I tried that…It didn't work" thoughts can bubble up very quickly. How long? Days? Weeks? Months?

Consider trying a new approach for at **least** two to three weeks. Yes, that seems like a long time, especially when your child is struggling. But unless you give it a few weeks, it probably won't work. Here's what will be happening in your child's head when you are trying something new, from week to week:

- Week One – "I guess she read a new parenting book. Here we go again. I'll just wait her out."

- Week Two – "This is getting pretty tiring. She usually gives up by now. Let me wait a little longer."

- Week Three – "I think she means it. She's not giving up."

Your mileage might be different, but I'm suggesting three weeks so that you don't give up too early. If you know you have a tough, persistent child, it would be a good idea to increase your persistence to five or six weeks. I know it seems that is a long time, but the longer you try a proven technique, the greater the chances that it will be effective.

M- Measure Effectiveness

Is it working? Are things getting better? Sometimes, this is very hard to measure. Other times, it's easy. If your student's grades are improving, then it's probably working. You can measure effectiveness based on two different criteria:

Am I being a better leader?

It's very tempting to focus on the student first, but I want you to focus on yourself first. And keep in mind this fact: Ultimately, the only person you can control is yourself. Since this book is about your doing things differently—changing your behavior—the first thing we should measure is *you*. Ask yourself:

Am I staying calm?
Or at least, Am I appearing calm?

As previously mentioned, most of the techniques in this book hinge on the assumption that you will be showing a calm exterior. You won't be losing your temper (at least as much), and will be coping with your own anxieties instead of placing them on your child.

Am I following the leadership style as well as I can?

Each of the three leadership styles has specific ideas and behaviors that will make them effective—and pitfalls that will make them fail if they're employed in the wrong situation. Review the leadership styles in Chapter 5 and grade yourself on how well you are doing at applying them.

Is my child changing?

You have been trying a new style, the Consultant, for example. It was hard at first, but you have stuck with it. You would give yourself a solid B+ on how well you are staying calm and following the style properly. Now, what do you look for with your student?

Better Grades

This is the most obvious way to measure progress. It's easy, but the problem tends to be that grades don't come in very often. But between report cards, you can always check with the teacher, the school, and even with your child about improvements in schoolwork.

Improved Study Habits

Most of the time you will notice a change in how your child is approaching schoolwork. This often happens before the grades improve. Improved study habits might look like:

- Less complaining

- A shift away from being defiant, sneaky, blaming, etc.

- Increased focus and energy on work

If things are improving, fantastic! Keep doing what you are doing. It's working. You are having a positive impact on your student. You are leading him, and he's responding. Pat yourself on the back and let your student know how impressed you are.

But Don't Do This...

Don't, at any cost, saying something like "I knew that if you just did what I said, things would go better." Nobody likes to hear "I told you so." Your kids definitely don't like it. In fact, some kids might, if they detect a hint of "I told you so," revert back to old behaviors. Independent-minded kids will not want to give you the credit for change. They want to give it to themselves. That's great! You should give it to them as well. Try complementing in vague ways that don't imply you had a hand in the improvement:

- "I'm really impressed by how hard you have worked."

- "This has been a very hard semester. But you stuck with it and it's paying off. Nice job!"

Avoid adding anything that suggests you were in some way responsible for their success. Doing so will backfire.

If things are not improving, you will probably know it. Don't despair. My first suggestion is to stick with it. While sticking with it, ask yourself:

- Am I giving it enough time?

My three-week rule of thumb might not be enough time for your particular student. Maybe it seemed like three weeks, but when you look at the calendar, you realize it's only been one! Change is hard, and time will seem to stand still.

Am I staying calm?
Should I refocus my energies on staying calmer?

This is a good time to ask someone you know who will be honest (not your kids!) about how calm you are actually being. Maybe you thought you were being calmer, but it's not enough to make a difference. I once had a father joke with me, saying, "I only screamed fifteen times this week! That's down from twenty the week before! Why aren't things changing?" Sarcasm. Gotta love it. But his point is important. An unbiased look might lead you to put more effort into mastering this "calm down thing."

Am I being true to the leadership style?

Each style has its pitfalls. Are you avoiding them? For example, you might have more experience in toe-to-toe confrontations than in shoulder-to-shoulder discussions, so you might unthinkingly resort to this behavior in a particular situation. Take a look at **how** you have been doing the Supporter, Consultant, or Boss and make changes if needed.

What Then?

If you feel you are doing your best and you have been doing it for over three weeks or so without any change so far, it's time to consider increasing the intensity of leadership, if indicated. For example, with the Unmotivated Student, I recommend you begin with the Supporter. If you have given it a good try with no results, it's probably time to add the Boss into the equation. You can still be supportive, but you are now including rewards and consequences in the mix.

OK, What Next?

If you have added the next level of leadership but to no avail, there are two core things to review:

Have I Missed Something?

Sometimes there are underlying conditions that are getting in the way that, regardless of how good a parent you are, won't change. These conditions could include:

- Depression
- Anxiety
- ADHD
- Learning Disabilities
- Substance Abuse
- Undiagnosed Medical Illness

One or more of these might be the underlying cause of the issues. If your child is dealing with one of these conditions, get some additional help. There are many professionals and organizations available to help with these problems. Check with your school counselor, who usually has a variety of local and regional resources.

Am I Really Being Calm?

Many times, we think we are being calm when we really aren't. I remember a father who was certain he was being calm, but when I watched him deal with a tough situation, he didn't come across as calm as he'd thought. Although he was no longer yelling, his non-verbal communication (body language) was not calm. Here are a few non-verbal ways we use to yell without raising our voices:

- Glaring
- Finger Pointing

- Head Shaking
- Exaggerated sighing
- Sarcasm (in this case, the tone of voice negates what's actually being said)

If you think you might be coming across angry, enlist the help of another person to observe how you deal with a tough situation with your child. For example, your spouse might be able to point out things you might not ever see on your own. When I work with a family, one of my major roles is to help people understand how they are communicating in ways that they might not even be aware of.

Don't Freak Out Chapter Summary

Remember: There are only three effective ways to lead your child when it comes to homework. Your task is to choose carefully which one will work the best: the Supporter, the Consultant, or the Boss.

Don't Freak Out Resource

To print a copy of the leadership chart/matrix for determining which style to use at what point, go to: www.reducehomeworkstress.com/exercises/matrix

CHAPTER SEVEN

Crucial Insights into the Student Mind

There's an old saying that babies should come with an owner's manual, so that we knew what to do and how to handle certain situations. I agree. Some of this "parenting thing" we do comes instinctively, but much of it doesn't. Sometimes, though, we tend to think that, since we were kids ourselves once, we don't need a manual. I don't know about you, but my memory of what it was like to be a kid has morphed and faded so much that I'm not really sure sometimes what it was like for me to be a kid. This chapter is a reminder of what it means to be a kid.

1. They Don't Learn from Their Mistakes

This seems self-evident, but over and over again we assume that our kids have some basic wisdom about life. They don't understand how much work it will require to be successful in life. Our kids don't have the wisdom to think about learning from what worked in the past and applying it in the future.

"I keep telling him to start projects early so he doesn't have to wait until the last minute, but he doesn't and I have to bail him out by helping the day before it's due. Why can't he just learn to get things done early?"

This is a question I hear quite a bit. Why can't he learn how to do it easier?

I think a big reason is that our kids haven't gained wisdom yet.

How do we gain wisdom? Usually by dealing with difficult situations over and over. It is the rare person who can learn a lesson the first time something bad happens. For most of us, it takes a few of the same bad decisions before we "get it." Our kids are the same. They will not learn from their mistakes—at least not at first.

Let me repeat that: *Our kids will not learn from their mistakes–at least not at first.* This is important to remember. It's much more difficult for children and teenagers to generalize about their actions and learn life lessons from them. They sometimes seem to make the same mistake repeatedly. But from their perspective (and limited frame of reference), each mistake is different. Thus, they have difficulty developing generalizations about their behavior. It takes a certain level of maturity and self-confidence to be able to say to ourselves: "Yep, that was my fault, and I've made that same mistake before."

What Should We Do?

a. Realize that learning from mistakes takes a very long time for many students. It won't come as quickly as we think it should.

b. Be patient. When we get frustrated with our kids when they are not "getting it," they will either just shut down or argue.

c. Be a Tentative Consultant (Chapter 5).

2. They Struggle with Delayed Gratification

What is one of the hardest things for kids? Delayed gratification. Kids want things right NOW, NOW, NOW! As they grow into their teens, that doesn't go away. It sometimes even gets worse in the teen years. A kid's focus is on the thing that will make them feel good immediately, whether it's a new piece of technology, something on TV, or something friendship-related.

If we think kids should naturally be able to delay gratification in order to get the "important" things done first, we've got another think coming! Kids are not wired that way. If we are honest about ourselves, most of us adults aren't actually wired that way, either. I know I'm not! In fact, delaying gratification is probably one of the hardest things for adults to do as well.

What is delaying gratification about? Hal Runkel, author of *ScreamFree Parenting*, shared this definition with me: Delaying gratification means giving up what I *want right now* for what I *really want* out of life. What do I really want? I really want to be about 25 pounds slimmer. What do I want right now? A double cheeseburger with fries. And a chocolate shake!

Now, you might be the type of person who has no trouble delaying gratification, but most of us can relate to how hard it is for a kid, after seven hours of school, to be able to say, "I'll do my homework first, then I'll play with my friends." Yes, some kids are naturally like this, but they are few and far between.

What Should We Do?

a. Stay "On Message." Being on message means to keep repeating the theme: "You will get to do the fun stuff after you have done the not-so-fun stuff." If we keep that message consistent, it will eventually have the effect we desire.

b. Gotta Do's vs. Wanna Do's. This was a phrase I heard from a parent. She would tell her kids that there are two types of things we do in life: gotta do's and wanna do's. Gotta do's are those thing we "gotta (got to)" do in order to be successful: chores, hygiene, homework, practicing, etc. Wanna do's are those things we "wanna (want to)" do in life: playing, computer time, TV, friends, etc. Gotta comes first, then Wanna comes after. It's a great, simple way to remind our kids about a big part of success.

3. They Feel a Tremendous Amount of Pressure to Succeed

My father, when he returned from Europe after World War II, was given a great opportunity by the United States. He had access to the GI Bill. The GI Bill gave a poor man the chance to go to college. So he enrolled at the University of Pittsburgh, along with thousands of other GI's and regular college students.

When he began taking courses, the classrooms were packed with students. Most courses were graded on the curve, which meant that only a certain number of students would get A's. The competition was, to put it mildly, incredibly fierce. My father used to feel sorry for the students who had to compete against those students who, although only a few years older, had spent the previous few years in combat. The regular students were just kids. The GI's were grownups who had experienced things that had matured them beyond their years.

"The non-GI kids didn't know what to do," my father shared with me. "When the competition for grades began, they didn't have a chance. Most of us, the GI's, were poor kids. We never dreamed we could go to college. Now that we were given the chance, we were going to fight for those A's."

Students these days are feeling pressure as well. Not as much as my father, but I think that no other group of students since the late 40s has felt such academic pressure. Justified or not, there is tremendous pressure to compete and get into a top-notch school. This pressure can be overwhelming for students, especially when it begins for some as early as elementary school.

This affects kids in many different ways. For example, I recently worked with a teenager with anxiety issues. He wasn't sleeping well, had no appetite, and was very edgy all the time. I asked him what he did for fun.

"Fun? I haven't had fun since 6th grade. Everything I do is focused on how it will look on my college application. I really liked acting, but I wasn't good enough to focus on that, so I gave it up to focus on stuff that would help me get into college. I used to love soccer. Now I only play it so that I can say I was on a varsity team. I don't do 'fun' anymore."

Pretty sad, isn't it? The problem is that this student isn't alone. I hear this type of response from many, many kids. The pressure they feel to succeed has taken the "childhood" away from many children.

What Should We Do?

a. Don't Pile On. If you know your child feels a tremendous amount of pressure, try not to add to it by reminding her about it. Do not to say things like, "You don't want to ruin your GPA, do you?"

b. Deal with Our Own Anxieties First. The fact of the matter is that you (and I) probably don't have the type of student who is Harvard bound. Or Stanford. Or MIT. If we assume that the only path to success is through an elite school, we are setting up a pressure-filled environment for our kids. I think it's important to look at our expectations for our kids and think about whether we are just piling on more pressure.

4. They Have a Lot Competing for Their Attention

Unless you have decided to raise your family without TV, computers, cell phones, and other technology, you know how many things are competing for your child's attention. Think about the following items:

TV	Cell phone	Internet/Video games
Computer	Homework	Friends

How do you think your child would rank these, from most interesting to least interesting? Homework will probably be last on the list.

A student once told me that trying to keep his attention on homework is one of the hardest things for him to do.

"It's always at the bottom of my list. I never find myself saying, 'I wish I could just do homework right now instead of playing this video game...'"

What Should We Do?

a. Unless you plan on going the no-technology route, accept the reality of the world we live in. We are raising our kids in a technology-laden society.

b. Most kids will have trouble managing their distractions on their own. They will need our help, but they won't want it. If you have a child who is having trouble managing technology, you will need to be the Boss and develop some IF-THEN rules (see Chapter 5).

c. Don't Freak Out! There is no real benefit to getting angry when you see your teen sneaking Facebook time while doing homework. She is not doing it to make you angry. It's just too tempting not to see what her friends are up to. Be the Boss, but don't freak out.

5. Their Friendships Are More Important Than Their Schoolwork

It doesn't matter how many times we tell our kids that schoolwork should come first. They won't agree. For many kids, especially teenagers, friendships are much, much more important than schoolwork.

"Andrea," 14, was in a constant struggle with her mother about the importance of friends vs. school. Andrea's grades would fluctuate with the ups and downs of her social life. The problem was that, whenever the friendships were going really well—or really bad—her grades would drop. When she was feeling really good about her friendships, she would spend too much time with them, whether personally or online. Whenever things were going bad, she would be "too depressed to do homework." The only time when friendships weren't getting in the way was when things were going "just OK" with her friends. Andrea could then focus on schoolwork. As a counselor, I see this issue quite a bit. The focus on friendships can be very important for many students. It's also necessary, in some respects. We are social beings. We are drawn to make connections with others and emotionally bond with them.

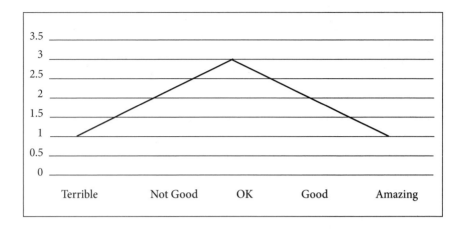

What Should We Do?

a. Don't say, "Schoolwork is more important than friendships." It won't work. Your kid won't believe you, and just saying these types of statements only creates more of a rift between you and your child. Ditto for these similar parent comments:

- "Your friendships won't help you get into college. Studying will."

- "I understand she hurt your feelings. But you'll feel better in a few days."

- "Why don't you take your mind off it by studying?"

b. Try being supportive and interested, without adding the "but" at the end of the sentence. For example: "I'm sorry it's going so bad with Julie. You must feel really bad." Stop there. Do not add anything else. You will be tempted to say something like "But you know that your test is tomorrow." Any influence you gained by being empathic will be lost if you quickly add the "but."

c. Delay the advice until long after the empathy. After you have let her know you understand how bad she feels, wait a while until you remind her of homework. By waiting, you will have a much better chance of being influential.

Although there are many more pressures kids feel, and many different ways to deal with them, these are the basics. The more that we keep these in mind, the more likely we will lead in ways that will produce the greatest chance for success. Because we are, first and foremost, leaders in their lives when it comes to schoolwork. The best leaders are ones who have empathy for their followers and find ways to motivate based on who the followers are (not what worked "back in the day").

Don't Freak Out

Instead, remember these three main points:

1. Our kids are still kids. They will do what kids do.
2. It's our job to lead them out of the things that will make life harder for them.
3. Next time you feel a lecture coming to the surface, try empathy instead. It will probably blow your kid away.

Don't Freak Out Exercise

1. Write down one pressure that your child is dealing with (e.g.: delayed gratification).

   _____

   _____

2. Write down one specific technique you would like to use next time you see it. For example: trying the gotta do, wanna do concept.

   _____

   _____

Don't Freak Out Resource

For a list of things to say instead of your old comments, go to:
www.reducehomeworkstress.com/exercises/instead-try-this

CHAPTER EIGHT

The Mistakes
We Make As Parents

Yes, I know—when do we NOT make mistakes as parents!? It seems I find myself making mistakes multiple times a day when it comes to parenting my kids. I have had to learn to not sweat the small mistakes that we all make as parents. In this chapter, though, I will focus on some general assumptions and mistakes we make about our kids that, if we think a bit differently, might yield some great results.

Mistake #1: The Heredity Assumption

What we know about intelligence is that many parts of it are inheritable. Generally, smart parents will have smart kids. So the likelihood of success is much better for kids born of smart parents. But there are lots of other factors working here. We aren't just talking about intelligence; we are also talking about achievement, which is a completely different story.

The likelihood that a high achieving parent is also going to have a high achieving child is statistically and genetically improbable. There are some traits that will transfer, especially intelligence, but the drive that has gotten you where you are in life probably has less to do with genetics than it has to do with circumstances. I hear from many successful people that the reason they are so driven to succeed is because they came from a family that was NOT successful. They were driven to be better than their parents.

My childhood is a case in point, but maybe not the way you would expect. My parents were born in the late twenties and survived a childhood in the midst of the depression, both in very poor parts of Pittsburgh. I was blessed in a number of ways by having them as parents, including the fact that they were both very smart. In addition, they were both determined to do whatever it took to be successful. My mother rose in the executive ranks at the Ritz-Carlton by her late twenties. My father returned from World War II and took advantage of the G.I. Bill to get three college degrees. They both continued to be successful, both in status and in finances. My mother was a very creative thinker. In fact, she invented the "wreath hanger," that piece of sheet metal that goes over doors so you don't need to use a nail on metal doors.

I was raised in an upper middle class home in suburbia, never having to worry about food, or rent, or clothes. My parents still had the "depression era" mentality, so we lived frugally, but comfortably.

I am thankful that I inherited their intelligence, but I did not inherit their drive and ambition. By the time I was in 7th grade, I was the classic under-achiever, getting the minimum grades necessary so that privileges weren't taken away. I had no desire to get straight A's. I would search for the sweet spot where I could do as little work as possible without being punished. It wasn't necessary for me to be "driven" as I was under the naive assumption that the comfortable life was easy to get. Of course I learned the hard way later in life why that's not the case, but I learned it on my own. No amount of lecturing from my parents convinced me that it was hard out there in the real world.

Today's kids are the same way. Many of us have given our children innumerable opportunities. I think it's a mistake to think they will just pick up those opportunities and run with them.

Try Something Different

The main tool you can use to help with this is to watch how you think about your kids and then ask yourself: "Are my thoughts about my kids helping the situation?" For example:

"I have given so much to my kids. They should understand and appreciate these sacrifices and work harder."

In my opinion, the anger that these types of thoughts produces cause more problems than solutions. It might be true, but focusing on how much we give to our kids and the lack of gratitude just makes us feel worse—and it doesn't help our kids at all.

Instead, try to adjust your thoughts to something that might be more productive:

"I'm concerned about my kid's lack of initiative. What I can do to increase it?"

Do you hear the difference? The first one is focused on our sacrifices and their poor intentions. The second one focuses only on their behavior.

By focusing only on their behavior, we can then be much more clear about possible responses. Calm, clear thinking produces much better solutions than worried, muddled thinking.

Remember: Passion and determination might not be hereditary.

Mistake #2: Forgetting That Your Child Wants to Succeed

Regardless of how bad a student might be performing, every child has an inherent desire for success. The problem is when we forget this. Every child wants to do better. Do you have a child that says things like: "I don't care. This is good enough." or "A C is average. Why can't you accept that I'm average?"

If you have a child that acts this way, don't believe him. Don't think that he actually believes what he is saying. He doesn't.

It is an act for your benefit.

Yes, we should always believe in our children, but we shouldn't always believe them.

When we believe IN our children, we are believing that they want to be successful in their lives.

When we believe IN our children, we remove any thoughts that they don't want to do well in life. But that doesn't mean that we always believe our children. When our kids tell us that they don't care about school, don't believe it. But it's important to understand that there is more happening in this situation than meets the eye.

So why is he doing this? Why is he saying he doesn't care?

Here is why:

He is trying to get you to back off or infuriate you to the point where you will either give up of lose your temper.

I have had many kids in my office say that they don't care...until their parents leave the room. It is then that they tell me that they actually do care. They just don't want to say that in front of their parents.

This is crucial for us to keep in mind when thinking about our kids' schoolwork. Every single one of them wants to improve—even if it *looks* like they don't.

For example, take a look at a typical conversation that happens in my office:

Mom: "You got another C in math. What do you have to say about that?"

Son: "It's just a C."

Mom: "What do you mean, 'just a C?' I thought you said math was easy for you."

Son: "A C is average, Mom. Can't you just be happy with average once in a while?"

Mom: "You are not an average student…"

Son: "Every parent says that. Every parent thinks their kid is above average. One thing I did learn in math is that everyone can't be above average!"

Now, I was very impressed with this kid's ability to keep up with his mother, to listen carefully to what she said, and find a way to turn the conversation so that he ended up looking good. Because for him, that is the main point of the exchange: to end up not looking foolish and to not lose face.

I then excused his mother for a bit and talked with him about the school situation.

"I hate it when she does that to me. She makes it sound like I'm an idiot and can't do anything right," he told me. "She always does this whenever I screw up. I know what she wants me to say, but I'm not going to give her the satisfaction."

I'm not going to give her the satisfaction.

This is the key to understanding the disconnect that happens when kids and parents discuss grades. We think what they are saying about their grades is actually what they think. Often times, it is not what they think. It's what they are saying at the moment to try to get the upper hand in the conversation.

I'm going to repeat that: Just because your child is saying "A C is OK" does not necessarily mean that he really thinks that. He is saying it because you are his parent.

As we continued talking, he told me, "Of course I want to get a better grade in math. I want to be an engineer and I know I need to do better. I don't know what happened this quarter."

"What do you think happened?"

"I think I was too confident. I did really well in Algebra 1 and I thought Algebra 2 would be really easy. And it was. I was getting good grades on tests and quizzes, but I didn't do the homework very much. I didn't need to, since I understood it so well. But that really hurt my grade."

"So what do you want to do different this quarter?"

"Do the homework, even if it's boring and I already understand the work."

"When your mom was in here, it sounded like you were fine with a C. Why didn't you say this when your mom was in the room?"

He paused. I could sense he hadn't really considered why he said one thing to his mother and then said something completely different to me. His answer was very telling:

"It's always a fight with my parents when it comes to school. They freak out so quickly when it looks like I'm slipping. I'm tired of saying, 'Yes mom, you're right. I'm a loser and need to do better.' I'm not a loser."

He paused, and I could sense he was thinking about something he might not have realized before:

"I just wish that it felt like we were on the same team. It always feels like a battle when we talk about school. And the thing about battles is that there is always a winner. And always a loser. And I'm pretty good these days at winning these battles," he said with a small smile.

This example is classic when dealing with kids who are struggling with something in their lives: What they tell their parents might not be what is really going on inside. It is so important for them to be viewed in a positive light by their parents, they will try to look good regardless of the situation. So, just because your child says that being an underachiever is OK, that is probably not what he is actually thinking.

Try Something Different

1. Try to keep in the back of your mind the fact that your child wants to succeed. Regardless of what is coming out of his mouth or what you see in his behavior, he wants to succeed. Your first job is to convince yourself of this. Because if we don't have an assumption of success, it is going to be very hard to be a leader in our children's lives.

2. Remember that when your child is talking to you, that fact that you are a parent is a huge issue. Any answer they give will be colored by that relationship. Never forget the power of parental judgment, good or bad.

Mistake #3: Trying to Be "In Control" Instead of Trying to Be "Under Control"

One of the best ways to help your child be successful in school is to be under control. Notice that I didn't use the term "in control," but "*under control*." The difference is huge. By "under control," I mean that *you* are in control of *yourself*, instead of someone else being in control of you.

When you are under control, you are saying that, regardless of what grades your child earns, regardless of how much homework gets done, you will decide how you feel and how you react.

The benefits of staying calm, regardless of what happens, are many:

Why do we want our kids to do well in school? Seems a pretty obvious question. We want our kids to do well so that they will be successful. When we can stay calm, we are increasing the odds of success. The calmer I am, the more likely my kids' energies will be focused on their own actions instead of mine.

If I am not calm, then their thoughts and emotions are focused on me, instead. I am making them responsible for how I handle the problem. So, instead of thinking about doing well in school for their own success, they think they should do well in school to change our emotions. I know that

I'm sounding like a broken record, but this point bears repeating. I have learned that when I am over reacting to a situation with my kids, I am saying it is their job to keep me calm.

The reality is that we cannot control our kids without it costing us, and them, dearly. A goal that most parents want is for our kids to have "self-control." If we are controlling them, then they don't have the chance to exercise self-control.

I remember a teenager, Jordan, who was in my office with his father. Jordan had brought home a D in science. The previous grading period he had earned a C. The grades were going downhill, and his dad was not happy.

"What else should I take away from you to get you to get a better grade? You've lost just about everything except the clothes on your back. How else can I make my point?"

"You made your point," Jordan said to his dad. "You are trying to control me. The only way to do it is your way. But I wonder if I made my point?"

"What point is that? That you want to fail?" said his dad.

"No. The point is that the more you try to control me, the more I will do it my way, even if it means getting worse grades."

This teen was what is called "oppositionally defiant." That means he will defy people by doing the opposite of what they want him to do. One of the biggest characteristics of kids who are oppositionally defiant is a strong sense of doing it their way, even if it hurts in the end. I knew what Jordan was thinking: In order for him to stay in control of his own life, he would not submit to his dad's way of doing things.

This is another example of the classic "cutting off the nose to spite the face" responses. Jordan is saying that it is more important that he be independent than be successful. In fact, later in the session, he said something stunning:

"Actually, I've been doing pretty good in History. We are studying the Revolutionary War. I think I've found my role model: Patrick Henry. Remember what he said? 'Give me liberty or give me death!' He basically said that being his own person—and not under the tyranny of an oppressor—is more important than his own life."

I was speechless. This kid had just aligned himself with a national hero and compared his father with King George! I wasn't sure what to do next. I knew that if I tried to convince Jordan that he wasn't being oppressed and his father wasn't a tyrant, he would tune me out immediately. My only hope was to help his father to consider how he would become less of a tyrant in Jordan's eyes—and more of a leader. I helped his father see that if he focused on being less controlling, the results would be increased responsibility with Jordan.

Try Something Different

When our kids see us more as tyrants and less as leaders, it's time to seriously consider what we are doing that gives them that impression. Sometimes it isn't what we are saying (content), but the way we are saying it (style). Consider becoming less angry and abrupt at these times and more conversational. Try to remember that your main goal is to get "buy in." You would like to convince your child of the reasons to try things your way. The words won't matter if the style doesn't allow the words to be absorbed. For more ideas about this, see the discussion in Chapter 5 on being a Consultant.

Mistake #4:   Dispensing the Wrong Punishment

Punishments are a tool we as parents have at our disposal, but sometimes we use that tool in the wrong manner. Just like a hammer used upside-down, if we don't use our tools properly, we are bound to do some damage.

For the third time this year, your son has waited until the last minute to begin a big term project. Out of sheer frustration, you tell him, "That's it. You are grounded for a month." After you calm down, you realize you went overboard.

Now what?

We have all been there. We let our emotions, instead of our principles, dictate our actions. Then we end up regretting our decisions.

Let's go through the decision tree to consider how to best deal with this situation.

You have two choices when you are being the Boss: Rewards and Punishments. The thing we know about getting homework done is that it is a "Start" behavior, so right away we know a punishment will be less effective than a reward.

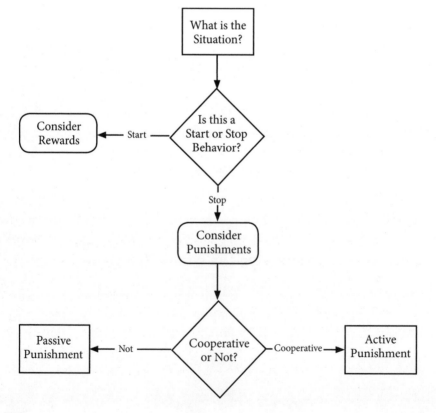

The second problem is that we are using a punishment that is longer than we would ever want to enforce. Do you really want a resentful, angry kid around your house for a month? One thing we know about punishments is this: They begin to lose effectiveness within 24 hours. Just think about how ineffective 24+ days will be!

Try Something Different

Let's assume you have gone overboard. What's next? I've seen many parents use the "you can work off the punishment" technique—with limited success. I am not sure exactly why, but I have rarely seen this approach work. I think the child knows what we are up to and will put in the minimum effort to get the punishment to go away. In fact, many kids will admit they like the "grounded for a month" punishment because they know the parents will not enforce it.

My suggestion? Just admit your mistake, tell them the new plan, and move on. I'm amazed at how many parents have trouble telling their kids that they have made a mistake. I promise that nothing tragic will happen in admitting you are human. In fact, I believe the more we admit our mistakes in front of our children, the more likely it will be that they will talk about their own mistakes with us. This would limit them having to save face with us.

Mistake #5: I Stopped Taking My Parenting Job Seriously and I Started Taking It Personally

We should take our parenting job seriously. Being such a major influence on a child's life is extremely important. If we don't take it seriously, we are not doing all we should for our kids. But when we take it personally, we have a tendency to get confused, hurt, angry—and we become much less effective.

Watching my son at football practice, I was reminded of a word I hadn't used for quite a while. The coach kept telling the players to lower their center of gravity. Problem was, the kids had no idea what he was talking about! They were about 9 years old and hadn't learned about gravity yet! What he was trying to teach them was to squat down a little lower so it would be harder for the opponent to push them around.

This got me to thinking about the concept of the gravitational pull our children have on us. I don't mean the real gravitational pull, but the emotional pull they have on us. If you remember your high school science, here's the concept in shorthand: the more massive object will have a greater pull on the less massive object. Therefore, the less massive object will tend to be much more affected than the more massive one. If you think of planets, it means the less massive object will begin to orbit around the more massive one.

We have been told, sometimes directly and sometimes indirectly, that our kids should be the most important thing in our lives. That the minute we have kids, our center of gravity should completely shift and we should begin to orbit ourselves around our children. And in the beginning, that certainly is the case. Their lives take complete precedence. They call the shots.

But as our kids move into the school years, I think our center of gravity should shift much more back to ourselves and not as much as it was on our kids. If we can find a way to balance the gravity issue so that our kids don't have as much affect on us emotionally, I think our ability to be strong leaders in their lives will increase a lot.

What happens if we don't shift our center of gravity? Then our kids become our whole lives. As Hal Runkel writes in *ScreamFree Parenting*:

"You cannot orbit around your child without giving her the distinct impression that the world revolves around her. And then you act surprised when she acts both selfish and incapable."

When we take our kids' actions too personally, it is because we have gotten a bit too emotionally close to them. One of the great things about being a human is balancing the fact that we are individuals, and at the same time we are driven to connect with others. But when we over-connect, we lose our sense of self.

Try Something Different

In the long run, the more we take our kids' actions personally, the more it will backfire on us—and ultimately on our kids as well. Whenever I start to feel parental anxiety creep up on me, I ask myself, "Am I taking this seriously or personally?" That one question has saved many a conversation between me and my kids. Plus, it then calms me down enough to carefully consider what my best leadership action should be.

Mistake #6: Misusing Rewards and Punishments

OK, I probably know what you are thinking: "Of course the reason for rewards and punishments is to change behavior. Why else would I do it?" Bear with me for a minute as I explain my take on this subject.

Our kids, especially the ones who have a tendency toward independence, have a very strong radar when it comes to what we want them to do. If they get the feeling that we really want them to do something, they will often dig in their heels to the point where they suffer.

"Dad can make me go upstairs to do my homework, but he can't actually make me do it."

Even though your child wants to do well in school, if you try too hard, it then becomes a power struggle, which you will lose.

In my opinion, the reason we have consequences for our kids is not to change their behavior, but to teach them about life. Life, in general, works like this:

If you do well, good things will happen. If you do poorly, bad things will happen.

Our job is to lead our children to an understanding of this. Our job is to create situations where we can teach this lesson. If they work hard and get their homework done, good things might happen. If they slack off and watch TV instead, bad things might happen. This is how we teach them about life.

If we keep our focus on how we should lead, instead of focusing in whether "it's working," there is a much better chance that we will stay consistent.

A favorite aspect of my work is travelling to different parts of the country and speaking to parents about the subject of schoolwork. And at least once during each seminar, a parent will respond to a specific piece of advice by saying, "I tried that. It didn't work."

This is what our kids love to hear. "I give up." They have waited us out and we have decided that a certain technique, punishment, or reward doesn't "work," so we stop using it.

Try Something Different

I am asking you to stop determining whether you are being effective by looking at the results too quickly. It's not your job. It's not your job to wear him down. It's not your job to "break" him. Your job is to teach him about life.

When you get your homework done by 8 p.m., for example, you get to play video games. That's the rule, whether it "works" or not. Try to begin measuring whether you are effective based on YOUR actions, not based on the immediate effectiveness of your actions.

Mistake #7: Making Decisions Based on Worries Instead of Principles

There are two major ways to base our actions toward our children: One is by considering our principles; the other is by considering our worries. Most of the time, when we parent based on our worries, we are going to be ineffective.

If you notice your child telling you, "Don't worry" pretty often, that's a sign you are basing your decisions on your worries instead of your principles.

I love the analogy used by University of Virginia professor Jonathan Haidt. In his book *The Happiness Hypothesis*, he uses the concept of the elephant and the elephant rider. The elephant is our emotional side and the rider is our logical side. Each side has its own strengths and weaknesses. The elephant is extremely powerful and, when steered in the right direction, can do great work. But when left to his own devices, the elephant can also be very destructive.

The rider, on the other hand, has very little power in comparison to the elephant. But the rider has something that the elephant doesn't: the ability to use logic and planning. When the rider uses his logic and planning to steer the elephant's energy in the right direction, good things can happen.

I would like you to consider that your worries are like the elephant, and your principles are the rider. When you let your worries run the show, without planning and logic, bad things can happen between you and your child. But when you use planning and logic to harness your worries in the right direction, good things can happen.

Don't Freak Out Summary

We all make mistakes as parents. How could we not make mistakes—it's the only way to learn how to do things the right way! Keep in mind that our goal is to stop making the same mistakes so often.

Don't Freak Out Exercise

Think of a schoolwork- related situation that you know is very stressful for you, and write it down here:

_____

_____

Now, think about the elephant, the pure worry side of you, and write down what the "elephant" side of you might do if there was no rider:

_____

_____

Now let's add the rider to the equation. Write down what you think would be the best solution when you have added the additional skills of planning and logic to the equation:

_____

_____

Hopefully, you were able to see that the chances for being an effective leader increase when you take the time to let the rider lead the elephant, instead of the rider holding on for dear life as the elephant barrels through the village!

Don't' Freak Out Resource

To learn more about how to keep our worries in check (and additional websites that discuss the elephant/rider concept), go to:

www.reducehomeworkstress.com/exercises/elephant

CHAPTER NINE

If They Only Understood...

As parents, we are constantly trying to teach our kids. We try to give guidance, show them the right path, and support their successes. We have the credentials to do this. We have two things that our kids do not: experience and perspective.

In our many years, we have accumulated a significant amount of perspective. However, when was the last time we used that experience to consider our child's point of view? Our kids face a tremendous amount of pressure in their lives. Academics, negotiating the social realm, and pleasing Mom and Dad are just a few of the pressures kids face. As adults, we have the luxury of understanding that these childhood pressures have a relatively short life. But we tend to forget the impact they have on the happiness and development of our kids.

"My mom has no idea what my life is really like," I was recently told by 13-year-old, Julie. "She thinks everything in my life is so simple. She's always telling me that it's not a big deal. Either she had an amazingly easy childhood or her memory is shot. I think it's the memory."

This chapter, for lack of a better term, is an empathy chapter. Regardless of how much you remember your youth, kids these days are dealing with things and feeling pressures that are very different from your childhood. Take a moment to turn off your own parenting pressures and learn about how kids feel about themselves and, especially, how they feel about their parents.

What Do Kids Really Want From Us?

I remember a story I heard from my friend and high school English teacher, Jenny Runkel. One of the writing projects she assigned was for her students to write on the topic of parents, and what they wish their parents would do differently. The results were eye-opening.

I decided to try my own experiment with a group of younger students. I was recently invited to an English class at a local middle school to talk about the process of writing a book. The teacher, Virginia Walker, and her class were a ton of fun and kept me on my toes the whole time. (A word of advice: Never give a 7th grade English class a section of manuscript to edit. They were ruthless! But in a good way, I suppose. They gave me a boatload of good ideas and ways to phrase tough sentences...) I asked this group of middle schoolers two questions:

When it comes to schoolwork, I wish my parents would…

When it comes to schoolwork, I like it when my parents…

And here are their answers. These are unedited, straight from the students' mouths!

I Wish My Parents Would...

- Help only when I ask for it.
- Don't remind me about my projects every five minutes. If I'm not freaking out, you don't have to, either. Even though I have only two days to finish a project it doesn't make me feel good when you freak out.
- Consider my work just as important as my younger brother's.
- Encourage me rather than scold me.
- Use positive reinforcement.
- Back off when I don't get an A.
- Compare me less.

- Stop making me redo math problems.

- Stop checking the school website because they think I'm lying about my homework.

- Keep my sister out of my room.

- My parents are the best. They allow me to do school work without interruption from THEM. My sister though drives me nuts when she interrupts me.

- Stop worrying about when I start my projects or when I finish them.

- Trust me a little more. Even though I don't want to, I *will* do my homework because I don't want a lower grade just because I was lazy.

- Trust me that I have time to do it later therefore not nag me.

- I wish my parents would help a little more. They help, but sometimes they're too busy, which is understandable.

- Know more about what I'm learning. Sometimes I ask questions they don't know and I have to wait for my brother to get home.

- Trust me and let me do what I want. I don't like it when my parent uses the word homework. It bothers me.

- Not tell me how much I need to do and when because it works out when I know how much I'm going to do, but not when they tell me how much to do.

- Get just a tiny bit more involved, like to tell me to check my agenda.

- Help me a little more with my work, because if I don't understand something and they help me, I seem to remember the things I learned better.

- Don't nag me – I know I need to do it!

- When I ask for your help, don't talk to me like I'm a baby!

- Don't tell me right when I get home from *SEVEN HOURS OF SCHOOL* to do more work. Give me a break, then I'll do it.

- Reward me more. I'm in all of the highest level classes, and I consistently get straight A's and A+'s, but they only say "good job." Other kids get monetary rewards or a night out to see a movie and go to their favorite restaurant, but I get nothing.

- Just let me take care of my own schedule and get my homework done on my own time, I know what I'm doing!

I Like It When My Parents...

- Congratulate me.
- Help only when I ask.
- Don't compare me.
- Don't brag about me (I feel like I must achieve a high level of success to please them).
- Explain something I don't get.
- Don't stress me out by saying that I have to get my homework done at a certain time so they can check it.
- Get detailed about the subject. When I ask for help they make sure I really understand without going overboard.
- Remind me about schoolwork, but not nag me. The more pressure is put on me, the more I want to run away from my work. I like that my mom will help me if I need it.
- Have knowledge about a subject and help me out.
- I like it when my parents help me when I need it, and make things look good but are not perfectionists.
- Let me be. I like when my parents just relax and trust me and let me do my work on my own.
- Never bother me unless I ask for help. I like it when they let me finish my homework when I want to finish it.
- Check over my agenda to see what I have and if I missed anything…

even if it's annoying when they do it.

- Stay away and let me do my work independently.

- I like it when my parents help me with my work because when I know that I did my work right it makes me feel good.

There are four major themes that can be seen in these comments:

1. Trust Me More.

2. I Want To Succeed.

3. Don't Freak Out.

4. I Want Your Help…Except When I Don't.

I will discuss each of these wishes, and why it is so hard for us as parents to live up to them. Why it's so hard to trust, stay calm, and help only when asked. I will then share some ideas that, I hope, will lead different results when it comes to these dilemmas.

Student's Message: "Trust Me More"

Trust me more. Trust that I have time to get the work done. Trust that I know what I need to do. Trust that I will do it.

One of the most important things our kids need to know is that we believe that they want to succeed, that they want to do the right thing, that they want to get good grades. I have not met a kid who starts his day thinking, "Today, my goal is to do horrible on everything at school. I really, really want to fail today!"

Parent's Dilemma: "If You Want Trust, Don't Lie"

Think about the top five characteristics you want your children to possess. Write them down here:

1. _____

2. _____

3. _____

4. _____

5. _____

I would bet that one of the traits you wrote down was honesty, or some variation. Honesty is something all parents universally want from, and for, their children. Have you ever met a parent who, when talking about his children, has said, "I really hope to raise a dishonest, sneaky, liar"? I haven't met a parent like that.

So when our kids lie to us, it's a blow to our self-esteem as a parent…our "parent esteem." Am I raising a liar? What if he keeps this up? What do his teachers think about him…and about me if I am raising a liar? So it's pretty easy to connect our trust of our children to whether they have earned it. In "real life," you wouldn't trust someone who lies to you, right? In real life, trust is slowly earned, and quickly broken.

We have a dilemma. Our kids want us to trust them more, and we want them to be more trustworthy. Be more worthy of my trust, and I will give it to you. Unfortunately, the parent-child relationship is full of these dilemmas. The following is a path out of this dilemma.

Solution: Believe in your children, but don't always believe them

Our kids need to know that we "believe in them." This is quite a bit different than whether or not we "believe them." They seem like such similar sayings:

Believe Me

Believe In Me

Just a difference of one word: **in**

When we believe **in** our kids, we acknowledge that we are on the same team as they are. We all want the same thing, ultimately: success for our kids. We want our kids to be successful. Our kids want to be successful. We believe they have the ability to be successful and that, with hard work, success is bound to happen. We believe in them. We trust that they want to do the right thing…most of the time.

On the other hand, there a many times when we probably should not believe our kids, for a number of reasons.

Sometimes they are just outright lying:

Dad: Did you finish your homework?

Child: Yes.

But in fact, the child has not finished his homework. Because he doesn't want to do it now, he is betting that dad will believe him. Therefore, this is an example of an outright lie.

Sometimes they are being sneaky:

Dad: Did you do your homework?

Child: Yes.

Dad: It looks to me like you didn't finish it.

Child: You asked if I did my homework. I worked on it. I just didn't *finish* it.

This is the future lawyer response. "It depends on what you mean by the word 'did.'"

This reminds me of a chat I recently had with a fellow dad. We were waiting for our kids to finish practice, and the conversation turned to backpacking, which I loved in my younger days. I mentioned that I had hiked many miles of the Appalachian Trail years ago, but never hiked the whole trail. The Appalachian Trail is a wilderness trail that runs continuously from Maine to Georgia. Hiking the full trail is a major badge of honor. Less than 10 percent of people who attempt to hike the whole trail succeed. So when he said, "Yeah, I hiked the trail. It was a lot of work. But I stuck with it," I was impressed. I had dreamed of hiking the whole trail, but had never had the time, money, or especially the dedication to pull it off.

But, as we talked about the trail, things didn't seem to add up. He had great stories of one section of the trail, but was very vague about other sections. After a while, a little grin started to show on his face. I knew something was up. After another minute, I asked him, "Um, did you really hike the whole Appalachian Trail?"

"Of course not!" he laughed. "That thing's over 2,000 miles! I could never complete something like that. I hiked about six miles of it one weekend. If was fun, but I can't imagine doing all of it!" He paused and then added with a smile, "You asked if I had hiked the trail. When I said yes, I could tell that you thought I had hiked the whole thing. But I couldn't help having some fun with you!"

I love this story. Not because it makes me look a bit foolish (that's probably the part I love least about it), but because it shows how quickly we can make assumptions and how quickly we can lead each other on. I assumed that when someone says they hiked the trail, they mean they hiked the whole trail.

I also assume that when my kids say they "did" their homework, it means they "finished" their homework. And you know what happens when I ASSUME, right?

Just because your child lies, it doesn't mean you can no longer trust him. The vast majority of kids will lie, at some point (or many points) about their schoolwork. This does not mean they are immoral. It means that possibly they have done something immoral. It does not mean you can no longer trust them. It means you had better be careful believing everything they say.

Fact of Childhood: Kids lie. Fact of Parenthood: It's our job to bust them when they lie and teach them why lying doesn't work. It doesn't mean we should stop believing in them.

Student's Message: I Want to Succeed

Throughout the student's responses, over and over again, is this theme: I Want to Succeed.

- I want to be successful, but I am not sure if my parents understand that.
- I know what I am doing, even if it doesn't look that way.
- I know it's better to get things done early, but sometimes I'm just too worn out.
- When I don't want to do the work, it doesn't mean I don't care.

I remember when my daughter was quite young, and, being the youngest and a strongly independent soul, her saying was, "I can do it myself." She would say it with joy when she accomplished something, and with anger when we tried to get her coat on to save time.

There are many things that get in the way of kids being successful in school. Difficult subjects, troubles at home, emotional or medical issues, learning disabilities, etc. The difficulty for kids is keeping motivated in the face of adversity. It makes it doubly hard for them if they think we don't know that they want to be successful in life.

Parent's Dilemma: If You Want to Succeed, Try Acting Like It

"He keeps telling me he wants to go to a top-notch college. But some days he acts like he doesn't care. Some days, I believe he doesn't care. I think he would be happy spending the rest of his life in our basement playing video games." Sound familiar? If so, then you are stuck in the dilemma of separating your child's words from your child's actions. If you really want to do well, then just do it! Am I supposed to believe your words—or your actions?

Solution: Never forget that your child wants to be successful

A child's ability to withstand difficult times is much less than an adult's. Our children's willpower tank (Chapter 11) is much smaller than ours. It's supposed to be. This is the time when they learn about facing adversity. This is when they learn how it feels to overcome a challenge, and how it feels when they don't overcome the challenge.

One way we can help them is to remember, especially during the tough times, that *our kids want to succeed*. They need to know that we believe in them. Regardless of what message your child might be sending you, she wants to succeed. Just keeping this in the front of your mind will do a lot in helping you lead your child. Avoid at all costs what I call "The Dark Side." The Dark Side, in this case, consists of those uncharitable, harsh, or negative thoughts about our kids' intentions. "He just wants to fail." "I don't think he cares at all." These thoughts, I assure you, will do more to harm your ability to lead than most other actions.

Student Message: Don't Freak Out

"Don't worry, don't freak out. Believe it or not, I can handle this." Over and over again our kids tell us this. When we freak out, we are basically telling our kids: I can't handle this thing you are doing. I don't have the ability to deal with this. You need to change so that I can calm down." The calmer we become, the more confident they will feel. We send a ton of messages when we are anxious, most of them are not so great. Go back and look at Chapter 1, Don't Freak Out, for a refresher.

Student Message: I Want Your Help...Except When I Don't

Interspersed in the messages are a number of times that students mention that they want help, that they appreciate it. But the clear difference is that they want it on their own terms. They don't want to do it on their own, but they want to be in charge of when they reach out for help.

Parent's Dilemma: If You Don't Want My Help, Do Better in School

It is hard to watch our kids want to do something on their own, when we just know there is a better, easier, or correct way of doing it. Isn't that our job? Shouldn't we help them do the best they can? The dilemma is that the more we help, especially when they don't want our help, the more resentful they will become of us.

Solution: Pull Back the Unsolicited Help by a Degree or Two

I remember when I was a Cub Scout and it was the time for the Pine-wood Derby. I was excited because my brother, an aspiring mechanical engineer, had this high-speed grease to use on the axles and wanted to show me how to use it and how to shape the car for the best aerodynamics. My dad was also very supportive of the grease, but told me I had to design and cut the block of wood on my own. Although he helped, my dad had me do all the work.

The final result showed that it was the work of an 8-year-old. The only good thing I could say was the paint job was pretty good. But I felt great about it. When we got to the race, it was clear that my car was the only child-created vehicle (do an Internet search on "Pinewood Derby" and ask yourself, "Are 8-year-olds really making these cars?"). But I didn't care. I could tell that the other cars were made by the dads, not the kids. I still remember one that had fake leopard fur on the driver's seat, perfectly stitched. But I had pride of ownership. Many of the other kids looked completely bored with the event. They had no investment in the results, since they had no investment in the process. I came in second in the race and about 54th in the artistic awards, but that didn't matter. That second place was huge because I EARNED IT, not my dad. It was My car.

I recently heard the quote "No one ever washes a rental car." Why? Because there is no ownership. The more kids own their work, and ask for the help only when it's needed, the better students they will be in the long run.

So we know our kids need help, but clearly, they want it on their own terms. They don't want to deal with all of their academics on their own, but they want to be more in charge of when they reach out for help. Which makes sense. Aren't we the same? Isn't unsolicited advice and help sometimes the worst kind?

So, in a nutshell, here is what our kids want:

1   Trust Me More.
2   I Want To Succeed.
3   Don't Freak Out.
4   I Want Your Help…Except When I Don't.

We will go a long way in leading our kids during their academic years if we keep this in the forefront of our minds. What do our kids want? They want exactly what we want.

Don't Freak Out Chapter Summary:

Keep in mind these four wishes, which so many of our children want from us. It's so important, in fact, that I would suggest you write them on a 3x5 card and tape it to your bathroom mirror!

1	Trust Me More.
2	I Want To Succeed.
3	Don't Freak Out.
4	I Want Your Help…Except When I Don't.

Don't Freak Out Exercise:

Take a few minutes to find out what your kids really think about their academics and how you, as their parent, can be helpful or unhelpful. Go to:
www.reducehomeworkstress.com/exercises/what-kids-think
to find an exercise that you can send to your children that will give them a way to let you know what they really think about school success, and a way to let you know how you can be more helpful.

Don't Freak Out Resource:

Go to:
www.reducehomeworkstress.com/exercises/3x5card
for a printable version of this card.

CHAPTER TEN

The Parenting FAQ's

During my parent trainings, one of the most popular parts is the question-and-answer period. It often continues in the back of the room for an hour or so after the presentation with a small group of parents who want to have their individual questions answered. I have compiled a number of the most popular questions and hope that these will answer some of yours.

Some Words of Warning

Be careful about jumping to conclusions when reading some of the answers. You might have tried something similar in the past, or you might think that it won't work for your situation. These are some of the caveats I occasionally hear.

"I've already tried that. It didn't work."

This is the most common thing I hear from parents when they aren't thrilled with a piece of advice. I am sure that you did try it, and it probably didn't work. There are two questions to consider at this point:

"Why didn't it work?"

In my experience, the number one reason why some academic advice doesn't work is due to the parent/child relationship. There are many emotional minefields in this relationship. Those minefields often are what prevent most academic advice from being successful. I have seen over and over again how well things begin to turn out when the parents have managed their own anxieties. If it didn't work in the past, it might have been because you were over-reactive emotionally, which got in the way of a successful outcome.

What exactly do you mean by "work"?

When we are talking about a machine, or a computer program, it's pretty easy to use the word "work." But when we are talking about another human being who is dependent on the outcome, saying "it doesn't work" takes on new meaning. As we discussed in Chapter 5, our goal in leading our kids is not necessarily to get them to do their homework (although that's a big desire of ours). Our goal is to lead them, to teach them about life. To help them understand that when you do good, productive things, good things usually happen. And when you are unproductive, bad things tend to happen. Even if the advice isn't having the desired effect, keep trying. There might not be another good alternative out there. Plus, many times it takes much longer to have a positive effect than we would ever imagine.

"That wouldn't work with my kid."

It might not work with your kid. I would never presume to know what's best for your situation, or for your kid. But I will ask you to possibly reconsider this opinion, especially if you have changed the way you emotionally react to your child. If you have significantly reduced the tension at home and have gotten control of your emotional reactions, you might be surprised at how things might work that you never thought would work.

"I don't have the energy or time to do that."

I hear you! That's one of the first things I ask myself when I consider changing something about my parenting. How much time and energy is this going to cost me? And do I have that much energy? If I don't, then can I consider readjusting things to get more time and energy (see Chapter 4). Most of my advice tends to ask less of parents than typical academic advice, so I hope you won't be having this concern very often.

"I think it's a good idea, but my spouse would never buy into it."

Try it anyway! I know I am swimming against the tide with this advice, but I think we spend too much time focusing on the importance of parents reading off the same page. It would be great to have buy-in from both parents, but it is by no means necessary.

If your spouse is strongly opposed to the idea, it is probably not great to try it. But if the issue is that you don't think your spouse will follow through, give it a try anyway and see what happens. A spouse will often be skeptical at first, but might support something after a bit of time.

The Questions

How do I deal with forgetfulness?

First things first. Let's go back to the student types. Forgetfulness is a characteristic of the Disorganized Student. Most kids who tend to forget assignments, or don't remember to turn in schoolwork, etc., don't actually do this on purpose. It is usually not willful misbehavior. Therefore, punishing forgetfulness doesn't tend to work very well.

"Don't do it FOR them, but do it WITH them"

Expecting a forgetful student to remember not to forget is an exercise in futility. For whatever reason, be it Attention Deficit Disorder, learning disabilities, working memory difficulties, or emotional stress or anxiety, the forgetful student tends to…forget. Our job is to do what we can to reduce its impact on education.

The first suggestion is to do the remembering *with* your child, not *for* your child. Examples:

Instead of checking the online homework assignments and then looking at the completed homework, require that your child pull up the website and cross-reference the completed homework **while you sit shoulder-to-shoulder and supervise**. Instead of doing the checking for the student, you are supervising the checking of the homework.

If he does the homework, but it doesn't get into the backpack to transport it to school:

Again, supervise the process. "Let's look at your desk. Is everything you need for tomorrow in your backpack? Show me. OK, good, now put the backpack next to the door. Good."

"How should I "check" my child's homework?"

This is a controversial question—one of the third rails of education. What is the right level of "checking" that parents should do with their child's homework? Here is my opinion:

It depends on which stage your child is in. For example, for Responsible, and Anxious Students, there should be little to no checking. There is no need to since they have shown they are diligent about getting the work done. An occasional look to see how things are going and what they are learning is fine. But being vigilant, especially with the Responsible Student, has the possible side effect of causing resentment. "Haven't I shown you I can do the work? Don't you trust me?"

For the Forgetful, Unmotivated, Defiant, and Disorganized Students, checking homework regularly is a pretty good idea. But I feel strongly, and most educators agree with me, that there is a big difference between checking to see whether the work is completed and checking to see if it is done correctly—or to your satisfaction. Most teachers do not want you to check your child's work for accuracy. They would rather see the mistakes that are being made so they know what areas need reinforcing.

I know this is hard advice to consider. It is difficult to let our kids go to school with incorrect work. We worry about what grade they might get and what that might mean for the GPA. But it is in these little, day-to-day opportunities where kids will learn the fact that doing good work means good rewards and doing poor work also has its consequences. When we insert ourselves into the equation, it has a tendency to cause resentment, resistance, and sometimes defiance. Letting the teacher teach is sometimes the best path to take.

Does that mean you allow shoddy work to go unchallenged? Absolutely not. If the work is clearly unacceptable, a blatant attempt at pulling the wool over your eyes or the teacher's eyes, then it should be considered incomplete. A redo is in order. If your child refuses to do the work over, then a consequence is in order as a response to that defiance.

If your child asks for help with a concept, or would like you to edit a written project, fantastic! But remember that you are now in the Consultant role. Just because she has asked for help doesn't mean you can help in the same way you might edit a company newsletter that an employee has produced. In addition to the words you are saying and the edits you are making, she is listening very carefully for your opinion of her. She is wondering, "Does Mom think this is good? Is she proud of me?" So remember to add a number of positive comments while being very tentative on the direct advice. Instead of "This sentence doesn't flow very well," try "I wonder if there's another way you can say this." "I wonder," "maybe," "you might want to consider," "maybe I'm wrong but…" are all phrases that tend to go a long way in helping advice be accepted.

How much should I praise my child?

A lot.

OK, I know, that answer won't suffice for this question, but I think letting our kids know how we are assessing their school performance is a good thing, and I don't think we do enough of it. Review the Supporter role for ideas about effective ways to praise.

One of the most important things is knowing the difference between praising ability vs. praising process. Some interesting studies have been done on the effectiveness of praising someone's intelligence vs. praising someone's hard work. There is much more power in honoring a child for how hard they worked on something vs. telling them how smart they are. The reason for praise is to underline the thing we want our child to do more of. Intelligence is somewhat out of their control. But working harder? That's something we can all do something about.

Rewards: Should I reward my child for good grades?

I have no problem with rewarding kids for good grades. We do it with our family and it tends to be a fun time when the grades come in and the rewards are doled out. But I don't think, at least for my family, this actually makes much difference in my children's performance. I think kids want to get good grades because it feels good to be successful.

But what if you have a child who's struggling to do better in school? Should you reward good grades? I think it can be very beneficial, but following a few guidelines can really help:

Be SMART. Decide exactly what you are rewarding. Many families use the SMART system for setting up a reward:

Specific – Jeremy will *complete his math homework* vs. Jeremy will do better in math.

Measurable – Jeremy will complete his math homework *and show it to me after completion.*

Attainable – Jeremy will complete his math homework and show it to me after completion. *Jeremy will do this at least 80 percent of the time.*

Relevant – Since Jeremy is struggling in math, this is a relevant goal.

Time Framed – Jeremy will complete his math homework and show it to me after completion. Jeremy will do this at least 80 percent of the time. *If Jeremy reaches this goal in the next two weeks, he will have achieved his goal and receive a reward.*

Why is it that when my child asks for help, it always ends up in an argument?

Maybe this scene is familiar to you: Your daughter wants help with a science assignment. "Dad, can you help me with this? I don't think I understand the Scientific Method." You are cautiously optimistic for a couple of reasons. One, this is the first time in quite a while she has asked for help. And two, you majored in biology, so the Scientific Method is right up your alley.

But you quickly begin to realize that you have stumbled into a trap. An emotional trap. A trap that neither you nor your daughter intended to set.

As you begin to explain things, your daughter begins to get more and more frustrated. Then, of course, you also begin to get more and more frustrated.

Daughter: "That's not how the teacher explained it."

Dad: "Honey, I'm trying my best."

Daughter: "That doesn't make any sense to me."

Dad: "I think I know what I'm talking about. I studied this for four years."

Daughter: "You're not helping."

Dad: "Why did you ask for help if you were going to snap at me the whole time?"

Daughter: "I thought you could help, but you just end up getting mad at me. As usual."

Dad: "Me, mad? You're the one getting snippy. You're on your own. I'm done helping."

Daughter: "Fine."

Dad: "Fine."

Full disclosure: This is the exchange I am sure will happen between me and one of my kids at some point. I studied biology in college and would love to impart my love of science and nature to my kids. I already get the glazed look when I try to explain the seasons, or gravity, or the age of Earth. I get the "Dad's going into his science nerd zone" look from them and then have to work hard to just let it go! But I digress…

The interaction above is typical of many parent-child interactions that go wrong. The problem is: It was doomed almost from the beginning. When a child asks for our help with schoolwork, we mistakenly believe that they want help with their schoolwork. So that's what we give them: help. And then it all blows up.

Here's the key to understanding this dynamic: In these types of situations, when your child is asking for help, she is very ambivalent about getting help. Now, I'm not much of a word nerd, but I did look up "ambivalent" because it is such a great word to describe our kids:

Ambivalent: simultaneous and contradictory attitudes or feelings (as attraction and repulsion) toward an object, person, or action

What are the ambivalent feelings in this situation? There are a number of them:

- I want help and I don't want help
- I am still dependent on my parents and I don't want to be dependent on my parents
- I know my parent has expertise in this and I want him to know I'm pretty smart too

Whenever there are strong ambivalent feelings in our kids, especially regarding schoolwork, it tends to be a big, big problem when we try to intervene.

I recently had the pleasure of chatting with Laura Kastner about this issue. Laura Kastner is a clinical associate professor at the University of Washington. She is the co-author of *Getting To Calm*. If you have a teenager, or a child who's about to become a teenager, this is a fantastic book to help you understand what is going on in the brain of a teen.

"It's a situation that's sometimes doomed for failure, especially with teens," Laura shared with me. "We naively think that this is a simple situation and all we have to do is provide help. But it's not. The kid is feeling two things very strongly: help me/I don't need help. If we can keep that in mind when helping, it will go a long way in decreasing arguments."

Suggestions:

First, keep in mind what role we are being asked to fulfill: the Consultant. Remember that the Consultant needs to be the Supporter as well, and needs to be tentative to be effective.

Daughter: "That's not how the teacher explained it."

Dad: "You are probably right. What do you remember about how the teacher explained it?"

Daughter: "That doesn't make any sense to me."

Dad: "Sorry about that. I'm not used to trying to explain this stuff. Should I try a different way?"

Daughter: "You're not helping."

Dad: "I bet that's disappointing. You were hoping I could help you with this."

Dad: (Dad pauses and says nothing more, but doesn't leave.)

Daughter: "Can you try to explain it again?"

Dad: "Sure."

In each situation above, Dad is not taking the bait. He is not getting indignant. He is not getting defensive, and he is not commenting on her irritability. He is defusing, defusing, defusing. He is giving her nothing to push against, which is the absolute best way to handle these situations.

What does a parent do if the student doesn't care about doing homework?

The first thing to do is: don't believe it. Don't believe it when your child tells you he doesn't care about school or homework. He isn't lying. It's just that he has gotten to the point where it's easier to try to convince himself that it's a lot easier to "not care" than it is to continue to try without success. I work with many, many kids who, during the first session with me, tell me they could care less about school. "It's stupid." "I never learn anything." Et cetera. These comments are especially strong if the student's parents are in the room.

But pretty quickly, usually within a couple of sessions, he will begin to tell me that he really does want to do well in school, but it feels impossible. It is a lot easier to say, "I don't care," than it is to say, "I can't do it."

The biggest thing the I Don't Care Student needs is the knowledge that we, his parents, are not giving up on him. He benefits hugely from the realistic Supporter and the Boss at the same time.

"I know you hate school. And if I was in your situation, I would probably hate it too and would want to just not care anymore, either. But I think you can do it—I think you can be successful. I know it's hard. I'm sure you aren't going to like this, but until you get your homework done, you can't spend time with your friends or be on the computer."

And consider getting a professional involved if your child is in the I Don't Care stage. Situations like this are very demoralizing for everyone in a family and the help, expertise, and encouragement of a professional can be very beneficial.

What should you do if your child forgets to turn in homework he has actually done? He does the homework, it gets to school, but it doesn't get turned in.

This is a variation of the Forgetful Student. So it's important to keep in mind that he is probably not doing this on purpose, and punishment is not going to help. In this situation I think it is crucial that we advocate for our kids. Having a teacher take a minute to ask him to check his backpack for the work, or to go to his locker to retrieve the assignment, is not too much to ask. Don't accept the statement from school professionals: "The only way he is going to learn to be organized is if he suffers from his forgetfulness." The research actually indicates the opposite. The more a child is punished for a non-willful behavior, the more likely that behavior will increase instead of decrease. The main point of education is to educate. If the student has done the work, it should be accepted and evaluated to see if he understands the material.

Reminders can help as well, but have your child set up the reminders.

- There are some great services available that can send a text message at a certain time as a reminder (this assumes your child has a cell phone and can use it at school).
- He can set his watch to beep right before class to remind him to get the history paper.
- He can write a sticky note on the proper notebook that says, "Turn in history paper."
- You can even supervise your child e-mailing his teacher with a message such as "I finished my history paper and it's in my backpack. But I might need some help remembering to turn it in."
- He could ask a friend in the class to remind him.

These are all things done by adults with memory issues. Let's teach our kids to do the same thing as a step on their road to school success.

How do you help them get organized, and how involved you should be?

It's a good idea to always begin by using the C.A.L.M. method. I am assuming that if he needs help getting organized, he's in the Disorganized Student category. And if that's the case, the best role for us is the Consultant.

I think parents should be significantly involved with kids who have trouble being organized for school. A child who is organized is a better learner. And leaving a Disorganized Student to his own devices is not going to produce good results.

Don't help. Lead.

And that means:

1. Never organize your child's materials for him. Instead, supervise it, but don't do it.

2. Set a specific organization schedule. Every week (depending on how quickly things get disorganized) do a regular AOP (Assess, Organize, and Purge). Pull out everything from the backpack. Assess what needs to stay and what needs to go. Organize the stuff that needs to stay. Purge the stuff that doesn't need to be there.

3. I would suggest using the AOP at school as well. Get permission to come in after school on a regular basis to AOP his desk, and especially for older kids, to AOP the locker.

4. Avoid ANY negative comments. "How long has this sandwich been in here???" "This is a mess!" etc. You are there to lead in organization, not to pass judgment or comment on it. If things are looking better than last time, by all means, be the Supporter.

5. Let me repeat: Do not do the work for him, just supervise.

Your goal in doing this is twofold. One, it is to help keep things organized, which will help him learn. Two, it is to show him, over and over again, the process of getting organized. Will he eventually start doing it on his own? Maybe. But even if he doesn't, we are teaching him a skill he can use when he is ready, willing, and able.

My son tells me that punishments do no good. In fact, he tells me it makes it worse. What do I do? I feel like just giving up.

If he is being the Forgetful or Disorganized student, he might be right. Punishments don't do much good in those cases. If he is being Defiant, don't believe him. He is trying to manipulate you. He throwing down the gauntlet and saying that you cannot influence him. Remember: The reason we reward and punish is not to change his behavior. It is about the bigger picture: to teach him about life. When you do good things, good things generally happen. When you do bad things, bad things generally happen.

I would suggest, though, that you take a step back and see if you are punishing in the most effective way possible. Am I doing it calmly? Am I over-punishing? Do my goals for him follow the SMART process? Often, it is not the actual punishment that the kid is reacting to, it is the yelling, the anger, the despair that is included in the punishment that is being reacted to.

Suggestion: In most cases, I would suggest that you don't respond at all to his remark that punishments are useless. Let it go. Some comments you might try, if you think they would help:

- "You might be right. But it's all I have."
- "I know. It's up to you whether you do well in school. But I wouldn't be able to look at myself in the mirror if I didn't do anything."
- "Whether it does any good is up to you. But this is what parents do."

As you try some of these suggestions, remember: Don't give up too soon! When we attempt something new, many kids will try to wait you out to see if you will throw up your hands and say, "I give up!" Don't give them the satisfaction!

Don't Freak Out Chapter Summary

This FAQ is in no way comprehensive, but just a few of the common questions I receive when speaking about the topic of struggling with schoolwork. I hope you see, in my answers, a pattern:

1. Stay calm

2. Assess what your child is doing

3. Pick a leadership style

4. Measure effectiveness

Don't Freak Out Resource:

Hopefully, in this chapter I have answered some of your questions about how to deal with specific situations in relation to your kid's homework. I am sure you have others. I have set up a community online at

www.reducehomeworkstress.com/message-board

to ask and answer questions and share stories of what has worked. Please stop by, ask a question, and share what has worked in your situation.

CHAPTER ELEVEN

Myth Busting – A New Look at Study Skills

There are so many things we have heard and "learned" in our lives that we simply accept as fact. The area of study skills and learning is full of ideas that, although ingrained in our habits, have been shown to be not helpful. In fact, some of these myths might even cause reduced learning. In this chapter, I will be busting some myths about study skills and showing you better ways to help your child.

As mentioned several times previously, one of the problems I hear over and over from parents is that the typical suggestions and advice they have heard doesn't work.

"I've tried that. I didn't work," is a refrain I have heard many times in my career. This got me to wondering about why some of the advice about homework doesn't work for so many students. This began my intense search into what we are missing when it comes to study skills.

The great news is that there are some amazing research projects happening worldwide, some recent and some a number of years old, that shed light on what works and what doesn't when it comes to homework.

Myth #1: Study in a Quiet Place

We have all heard this one a million times. Find a quiet place to study, free from distractions—that way, you can focus on your work. This piece of advice works for many people…except the people it doesn't work for.

My theory is that this piece of advice is perpetuated by those people who benefit from having a quiet place to study. (Their reasoning might sound something like "Since it works for me, it should work for everyone.")

What recent research is finding tends to put this idea to a big challenge. In fact, many kids do much better when there is some type of sound around them. For some kids, the idea of studying in a quiet place will drive them nuts. It's quiet, too quiet, for them.

Some kids would rather do their schoolwork in the kitchen, or the dining room near "the action."

TV still tends to be the deal breaker. Although not yet certain, it's pretty clear that television provides too much of a distraction and doesn't enhance learning. But music, background conversation, or similar white noise might be just the ticket for certain learners.

However, if your student is the type who will benefit from a quiet place, she will probably seek that out on her own.

Myth #2: If You Try Harder, Your Willpower Will Increase

A group of researchers conducted a fascinating experiment on willpower, and the results were pretty surprising.

Imagine that you are a subject for a research study. You enter a small room with the researcher, and she asks you to have a seat in front of a table. She then sets two plates on the table. One plate has six or seven radishes. On the other plate are six or seven freshly baked chocolate chip cookies (emphasis on "freshly baked": they just came from the oven, still warm and smelling incredible!) Since you are a pretty smart person, you've already figured out that you will probably be randomly assigned to eat either the radishes or the cookies. You are hoping for the cookies!

The experiment has already begun.

You were right, but you also were unlucky. You were randomly assigned the radishes. Bummer. You are told to eat as many of the radishes as you would like, but to not touch the cookies. The researcher then leaves the room, telling you she will be back in 10 minutes. Temptation now begins. Do I eat the cookies? She told me to leave them alone. But they smell *so* good. But I want to be a good research subject. Back and forth your mind goes while you nibble on a bitter radish.

Ten minutes finally drags by and she escorts you to another room, where she asks you to attempt to solve a geometric puzzle, tracing a complicated shape without lifting your pencil or tracing again over a line. Unknown to you, this puzzle is designed to be impossible to solve. Eventually, in frustration, you give up, thinking that you have failed the experiment.

While you were working on the puzzle, the researcher was timing how long it took you to give up. She added your time to the group of other radish eaters and compared the time with those participants who were told to eat cookies, as many as they wanted.

This last step, how long before a person gives up, is what was being measured. The cookie eaters try and try and try. On average, they take 19 minutes before giving up. The radish eaters? They last an average of 8 minutes! The radish eaters give up 11 minutes earlier than the cookie eaters! In the research field, that is a HUGE gap! Why?

The reason: The radish eaters ran out of willpower. They ran out of self-control. For 10 minutes in the first room, they had held back their impulses, keeping themselves from indulging in the cookies. So, by the time they got to the next room and were challenged again to control their impulse to give in (or give up), they gave up much quicker.

The radish eaters had depleted their ability to control themselves. Because what we now know about self-control is this:

Self-Control is more like a fuel tank than a muscle. It can become depleted. And when it's depleted, it is very hard to have any willpower.

When you think about it, this makes a lot of sense. Think about when you have had a hard day and you come home to your family, how easy it is to snap at them. It's because we have tapped most our reserves of willpower during the day.

What does this mean for your kids? It means that for many, many kids, coming right home from school and getting their work out of the way will seem like an impossible task. It's because their willpower tank has been exhausted at school and they have nothing left when they get home. Some kids can take 20 or 30 minutes and are ready to go. Many kids, especially ones who might be struggling to get their homework done, will probably need to take much longer, possibly an hour or two.

Trying to get your child to get the homework done when their willpower tank is empty is an exercise in futility. You can probably get them to sit at the desk, and you can probably get them to hold the pencil, but their brain is not engaged. I've heard of battles of wills where the child sits for hours without doing work.

"I can't do it. My brain just feels like it's dead," is the statement of a child whose willpower tank is empty. What looks like laziness is often plain and simple exhaustion. Going to school, for most kids, is exhausting. What is exhausted? Their willpower.

So the idea to keep in mind is this: Kids need breaks, sometimes longer than you realize. And hopefully you also remember that you need breaks as well, because it's the time of day that your child's willpower tank is empty is when yours is empty as well.

Later in the chapter, I will give you a great tool that can be very helpful in managing the willpower tank. It is called The Pomodoro Technique.

Myth #3 – Study in the Same Place at the Same Time Every Day

This myth, that routine schedules are best for learning, is still being perpetuated as recently as a study skills book published in 2010. Create a study spot for your child, have all of the necessary materials at the same place, and have a routine that allows your child to do homework at the same time every day.

In my opinion, this is a recipe for failure, for more than one reason.

First, most research about learning is telling us that students learn better when they learn and study the material in many locations. We have actually known this for over 30 years! In one experiment, college students who studied a list of 40 vocabulary words in different rooms—one windowless and cluttered, the other modern, did much better on a test than students who studied the words twice, in the same room. Subsequent studies have agreed with these results. By the way, the initial study was done in 1978! This is an example of the tenacity of certain ideas, even if there is little evidence to back them up. Possibly one of the reasons it has remained so popular is that doing things in the same place/same time is very convenient for us parents!

My suggestion: Add variety to the places where studying is happening. If your child can read in the car without getting carsick, great. Kids spend much more time in the car these days than in years past. It's a great place to study vocabulary, spelling, do math homework, etc. Cooking dinner? Have your child come in with his flashcards and quiz him while he helps fix the meal. Expand the variety of places where learning can happen.

The second part of the myth, studying at the same time every day, has no evidence that it does any good for increasing student success. Some articles say it will produce a routine that then can be counted on, which will then increase the chance of doing better.

I am pretty convinced that most of the articles suggesting this are written by authors who are naturally very organized and think their routines will work for everyone. My experience with so many struggling kids tells me that we are setting them up for failure by trying to get them to study in a way that is strongly against their nature. I have rarely seen a child who doesn't naturally gravitate toward a schedule and then adopt it wholeheartedly. But the process needs to come naturally; it should be encouraged, not dictated.

This advice is additionally hard because, if you live in a typical modern family, no two days of the week are the same. Telling parents to have the same routine each day of the week is a double failure. One: It doesn't work because our lives are too varied and fragmented, and two: It's another thing for parents to feel guilty about.

Myth #4: I Need to Help My Child Based on Her Learning Style

I recently had the pleasure of visiting a local elementary classroom where the kids were having a great time with a spelling project. They had gone outside and collected twigs and were now in the process of gluing the twigs to construction paper in the shapes of letters to make their spelling list. It was a fun, messy project, and I wished I'd had a teacher like that when I was a kid. When I asked her about the activity, she told me it was to help the kids learn by using their kinesthetic sense of learning. By touching the letter shapes, it will help them learn their spelling words.

"Plus, it's a lot of fun! We have been cooped up in this room too long with bad weather. We needed to get outside for a while."

I could tell that it certainly was fun. But I was very skeptical that the kids were actually learning anything about their spelling words by touching the twigs.

For the past 20+ years, a certain theory of learning has become so widespread that most people accept it as fact: Students have specific learning styles. Most of the time, we talk about three major styles: Auditory (hearing the information), Visual (seeing the information), and Kinesthetic (touching, moving, etc.). The theory then states that each student has a major strength in one of the areas, and that it is the job of the parents and teachers to help students learn based on their area of strength.

There is a bit of truth to this myth. Just like in any comparison to others, we all will fall on a bell curve based on where our strengths lie. But most of us will fall pretty close to the center line.

So, if the theory is wrong, why is it that everyone thinks it's right? One reason is that almost everyone believes it, not just educators. Up to 90 percent of college students know about this theory and accept it as fact (Willingham, 2009). However, there is some truth to the theory. Some of us have a specific method for learning that is better than others. But most of us still fall within a pretty narrow range of average.

In Dr. Willingham's words (Willingham, 2005):

"What cognitive science has taught us is that children do differ in their abilities with different modalities, but teaching the child in his best modality doesn't affect his educational achievement. What does matter is whether the child is taught in the content's best modality."

What this means is that the method of teaching should be predicated on the subject matter, instead of trying to customize the teaching to the student who is being taught. For instance, spelling is taught best through the visual channel: seeing the words on the paper. When spelling is taught via the auditory channel (hearing the words), learning declines. What is remembered is the tone of voice, not the actual words. Try teaching a child the shape of his home state by describing it verbally! It's very hard. Even if you give a child a piece of wood shaped like the state, he will still be remembering it via his "mind's eye." He will be making a picture of it in his head.

What does this mean to us as parents? Mainly, relax about trying to figure out your child's learning style. Figuring out the learning style won't make much of a difference when it comes to actual learning. Furthermore, don't try to structure your child's study routine based on his learning style. It tends to be not as helpful as you might think and saps your-already depleted amount of willpower.

New Ways to Look at Study Skills

So, now that I have removed some of the imbedded tools and theories regarding study skills, what are we left with? Actually, I haven't really taken away anything. I am assuming that many of the ideas above are ones you have tried without much success. So let me tell you about a few things that might tip the scale more powerfully toward success.

Little Pieces, Bit By Bit

I think most of us know this intuitively, and recent research is telling us we were right. Cramming for tests is about the worst way of remembering information. We learn much better when we "small chunk" information instead of trying to learn it all at once. Helping our kids "chunk out" studying can pay big rewards for them. One way to do that is, at the beginning of the week, add small amounts of time to their assignment books to study for a test or quiz that is coming up, instead of adding an hour the night before the test. Then, the night before, have them spend a few minutes quickly looking over all of the material, then go to sleep. The results will be much better than trying to cram it in at the last minute. So remember, Don't Cram, Chunk Instead!

Stop Calling it "Homework"

This is a small, but very significant thing you can do to help during homework time. So many of the kids I work with struggle with long-term projects. One of the main reasons for this struggling is that they don't think about the projects when they think about "homework."

When they're asked, "What do you have for homework?" they often respond with a list of what is due the next day. They don't mean to be sneaky. It's just that they don't think about the long-term projects. I suggest parents ask the question a different way, and then add another question:

- "What schoolwork do you need to do tonight?"
- After your child answers, then ask:

- "How about any long-term projects, papers, or studying for tests?"
- This helps jog their memory, and if done gently, doesn't create conflict.

Distracted? Make a Tomato Work for You

This is one of the most unusually named techniques out there, but I love it. "Pomodoro" is Italian for "tomato." The person who developed this technique, Francesco Cirillo, used a kitchen timer in the shape of a tomato. Since he's Italian—Pomodoro!

The concept is pretty simple:

Look at the tasks you want to complete, assign an estimated amount of time for each task, and split the time into equal periods, usually anywhere from 10 minutes to 30 minutes. Francesco calls each of these time segments "pomodoros." After each pomodoro, take a 5–10 minute break.

Here is how I teach it to my clients:

1. I have the student review all of the work he will need to complete that evening. I ask him to list each item.

2. Then, next to each item, I have him estimate how much time each section will take. One page of math? Twenty minutes? I have him write down the times next to each activity on the list. Then I ask him to think about any long-term projects and how much time he should spend on those that night.

3. We then break each time period into pomodoros. A pomodoro is a period of time you think your child can try to keep sustained attention without getting distracted too many times. Here are some amounts that you might want to consider based on his or her grade level:

Elementary School	10–15 minutes per pomodoro
Middle School	10–20 minutes per pomodoro
High School	15–20 minutes per pomodoro

I would not suggest that you use more than 20 minutes for each block of time. Keep in mind that each block of time is called a "pomodoro."

Put the number of pomodoros next to each task. For this example, the student selected 10- minute pomodoros. We then cross out all of the extra pomodoros, rounding up to the next pomodoro. For example, if a task takes 15 minutes, we will give it two pomodoros.

Task	Minutes	Pomodoros	
Math, page 23 1-19	10	⏱ ⏱ ⏱ ⏱ ⏱ ⏱	||||
Study Vocabulary	15	⏱ ⏱ ⏱ ⏱ ⏱ ⏱	
Reading	30	⏱ ⏱ ⏱ ⏱ ⏱ ⏱	
Practice Drumming	20	⏱ ⏱ ⏱ ⏱ ⏱ ⏱	
Science Worksheet	15	⏱ ⏱ ⏱ ⏱ ⏱ ⏱	
History First Draft	60	⏱ ⏱ ⏱ ⏱ ⏱ ⏱	

4. Now, the real power of the technique begins. The student begins his homework by setting the timer for 10 minutes. He then begins the work. Every time he finds himself off topic for more than a few seconds, he puts a tic mark in the last box and then gets back to work. Each time he notices he is off topic, a mark goes in the box and he gets back to work.

   The power of this lies in the fact that he is monitoring himself and tracking his own distractibility, then getting back to work. Over a short period of time, he will find that the number of tic marks decreases as he gets better and better at redirecting himself.

5. At the end of the pomodoro, when the bell rings, he re-sets the timer for 5 minutes and does something unrelated to schoolwork. If he's a "twitchy" kid, he will get up and shoot some baskets with his nerf

ball. If he's a gamer, he will play a game that's easily stopped after a few minutes.

6. When the bell rings again, he will set the timer for 10 minutes and start his next pomodoro, keeping track of his distractions along the way.

I have had very good success teaching this technique to students. It's fun, a bit silly, and very simple. And most importantly, it works.

Don't Freak Out Chapter Summary

I hope this chapter has given you a new way to look at some old problems, and will open up some easier ways for your child to finish homework. There are many ways to study, and it might be that the way you study won't work for your child. That's OK. Just try something different.

Don't Freak Out Exercise

Download a Pomodoro chart form my website at www.reducehomeworkstress.com/exercises/pomodoro and use it with your kid today!

Don't Freak Out Resource:

Daniel Willingham is a cognitive researcher at the University of Virginia who has done a great deal of research on this subject. He has a very readable blog at www.danielwillingham.com. Plus, he has some great videos on YouTube explaining this myth.

Final Thoughts

Well, I have to tell you I am impressed! You made it all the way to the end of the book! I rarely make it to the end of self-help books since I tend to skip around quite a bit. If you have made it this far, I want to thank you. The effort you have made to learn these ideas will pay great dividends in the future of your children.

I hope you stay in contact with me. I am easily reached via e-mail at neil@neilmcnerney.com

And twitter at: @neilmcnerney

And facebook at: www.facebook.com/reducehomeworkstress

My parting advice to you is this: Stay Calm. Don't Take It Personally.

Thanks!

Neil

Acknowledgements

Writing this book was exactly what I thought it would be: The easiest thing I have done—and the hardest thing I have done. Depending on the day (or the week), it either flowed like water or was stuck like granite. There are many people I would like to acknowledge who helped it along and kept me going when the motivation was, well, granite-like.

I would like to start with the person who, above all else, made this book happen: my wife, Colleen. She told me for many years that I needed to start writing down these parenting ideas and make a book out of them. And I would answer, "Sure, some day." Colleen's support and patience through this process has been amazing. The only way I was able to write this book while, at the same time, holding down a full-time counseling and training job, was knowing that I had the support of Colleen. Never did she express resentment or frustration with the process. Her words were always supportive and encouraging. Thank you, Colleen, for making this book happen. It literally wouldn't have happened without you.

To my son, Max, who was my first experimental subject when it came to using this approach. Although I have given much advice to many parents, actually taking my own advice was something completely different. Max, though, made it easy. His patience with me and dedication as an occasional co-author has been very helpful.

To my daughter, Shannon. Her strength and dedication to anything she does is awe inspiring. Whether it's soccer, academics, or getting back up on an unruly horse, she is a testament to hard work and dedication. Shannon also makes parenting very easy through her dedication. I also thank her for her unconditional love and support through this process, never once holding a grudge when I wasn't around.

To Lauren Kruck, my editor and administrative guru, who keeps the wheels from falling off around me.

To Hal Runkel, author of the New York Times Bestseller: *ScreamFree Parenting*. Hal's ability to take very complicated concepts of family systems theory and find ways to communicate them is second to none. Hal has been a great teacher on how to use small phrases and words to create significant change. I am honored to be involved with screamfree.com and hope our relationship continues to create calm in families.

To Tom Phelan, PhD, author of many fantastic books including *1-2-3 Magic*. I have been using Tom's ideas in my work with families (and with my own family) for twenty years. Tom has been very helpful in sharing insights into the writing process and has been a great support.

Thanks to Amy Collins and her staff at New Shelves Distribution. Her no nonsense approach and incredible integrity has been a welcome change. She has helped this new author understand the nuances of the publishing business and has been great at follow-through.

Thank you to all of those who agreed to be advanced readers of this book. Your feedback has been fantastic and has helped me figure out how to turn an idea into a message that can be read easily. I hope to continue to rely on your help in the future.

Blue Ridge Middle School 7th Grade Honors English Class, Chapter 9 is dedicated to you, since most of it is your work! It was an amazing experience to partner with such a skilled-beyond-their-years group of 7th graders to develop a chapter that might help parents truly understand what is going on with their children. Your honesty and insight was fantastic. And your editing was some of the best I have ever seen! Imagine a class of 20+ students, each with a laptop open, doing a crowd-edit of one document! Thank you Max McNerney, Matthew Slook, Robbie Feconda, Drew Hunter, Emma Rodriguez, Claire Deaver, Peyton Major, Kaitlyn Harper, Alisa Moortgat, Lexi Randall-Kelly, Will Elias, Suzy Janney, Leila Francis, Ally White, Marguerite Keane, Rohma Aziz, Caroline Richards, Kiran Sweatte, Madison Telles, and Megan Gannaway.

And especially to their teacher, Virginia Walker. Ginny was a great support in having me become a part of her class. I only wish I'd had such a great

English teacher in middle school! Ginny was a great help in being an advanced reader and fine tuning many passages to make them more readable.

Bill Hornbeck, neighbor, friend, and branding guru, who developed the subtitle of this book while we were out splitting wood. Within 30 seconds of me telling him about the book he quickly told me the subtitle, "It seems this book is a parent's guide to helping out without freaking out." I quickly went inside and wrote that down!

Dorothy McNerney has been the support that every son wishes he had when taking a new risk in his life. She has been tremendously encouraging throughout the whole process. I couldn't have asked for better support from a mother than she has been. Books have always been a huge part of our family. And yes, I also wish Dad were here to see his son as an author.

Eric McCollum, Program Director for the Marriage and Family Therapy Graduate School at Virginia Tech, has been a great inspiration and source of confidence throughout the years. Eric's belief in my abilities has allowed me to grow in confidence as well. It has been an honor to be involved with such a great graduate faculty.

Bill O'Hanlon, author of countless books, has been a source of inspiration for over 25 years. I have appreciated every single training and conversation I have had with him. Bill has been one of the major reasons I was able to move from the thought: "I could write a book," to the plan: "I will write a book," to the result: "I have written a book." As Bill often says, "Write is a verb."

Jon Kaplan, Managing Director of The ScreamFree Institute, has been an encouragement and friend throughout this process. His gentle leadership has helped me become not only a better leader, but a better person.

To all the families I have had the pleasure to know these past 20 years; this book is due to their hard work and dedication to themselves and their futures. These families shared countless examples and pieces of advice. My duty is to share those great pearls of wisdom so that others can gain from them.

(Endnotes)

1. Baumrind, D. (1966). Effects of Authoritative Parental Control on Child Behavior, *Child Development, 37(4)*, 887-907.

2. *http://www.newsweek.com/2010/07/10/the-creativity-crisis.html*

3. Faber, Adele, and Elaine Mazlish. *How to Talk so Kids Will Listen Video Series*. Rye, NY: Faber/Mazlish Workshops, 1996.

4. Levy, Ray, O'Hanlon, William, and Goode, Tyler. *Try and Make Me!: Simple Strategies That Turn off the Tantrums and Create Cooperation*. [United States]: Rodale/Reach, 2001.

5. Runkel, Hal. *ScreamFree Parenting: The Revolutionary Approach to Raising Your Kids by Keeping Your Cool*. Broadway Books, 2007.

6. Willingham, Daniel. *Why Don't Students Like School: A Cognitive Scientist Answers Questions About How the Mind Works and What It Means for the Classroom*. Jossey Bass, 2009